CUT THE SUGAR

You're Sweet Enough

COOKBOOK

Ella Leché

Andrews McMeel
Publishing®

Kansas City · Sydney · London

To my sweet daughters,
Gabriella & Amelia

CONTENTS

FOREWORD

How to Enjoy Your Vices

I am a major proponent of people enjoying their vices. I often ignore whatever medical advice happens to be in vogue because research has shown that it's not always necessary to be so cautious. For example, the science is very clear, and has been for decades, that salt (excluding table salt), tea, and even chocolate are health foods.

Excess sugar is not healthy. I'm not worried about the sugar normally found in fruit, or even the sugar found in small amounts of dark chocolate. (Go for quality, not quantity.) Rather, the problem is the approximately 140 pounds of sugar per person, per year, dumped into processed food. Excess sugar consumption not only can cause anxiety, depression, fatigue, and weight gain, it also is a major trigger for autoimmune disease, diabetes, cancer, schizophrenia, and heart disease.

The answer? It is not to make yourself feel guilty about enjoying pleasure. The answer is to learn how to enjoy pleasure healthfully. This is what *Cut the Sugar, You're Sweet Enough*, the excellent book by Ella Leché, does. Once you learn the helpful life skills in this book, you'll be able to have your cake—and enjoy it, too!

—Jacob Teitelbaum, M.D., author of *The Complete Guide to Beating Sugar Addiction,*
From Fatigued to Fantastic! and the *Beat Sugar Addiction NOW!* series

my story

I used to think I had good eating habits. I ate salads, I drank water—but I also consumed too much of foods that eventually almost killed me. Empty carbs like wheat, gluten, and especially sugar were doing my body more harm than good. But I didn't know that, and I wouldn't know that for years to come.

I spent my childhood in Poland, where I ate mostly all organic, local, seasonal foods. We lived in the countryside and grew our own food on a small family farm. Our vegetable garden and numerous fruit shrubs and fruit trees around the property provided us with plenty of food to live on, nearly year-round.

My mom made every meal from scratch and we six children sat around a big dinner table. She would bake each Sunday, of course. It was instant joy to bite into something delicious made with care and love. We kids were often assigned tasks to help in the kitchen—mixing batter, peeling potatoes, chopping vegetables. I was good at observing how things were done, and I started to bake my first treats when I was eight or so.

Then we moved to Canada when I was ten. My mom, a sudden widow, was looking for a better life for her kids. Times were rough, but we always had a great home-cooked meal in front of us. I remember my mom waking up before dawn and cooking so that when we came home from school, dinner would be ready for us while she was still at work.

But meanwhile, through friends, TV commercials, and grocery store displays, we kids were introduced to sugary processed foods like Cinnamon Toast Crunch, Pop-Tarts, and Quik Chocolate Milk. We wanted a say in what foods we ate, and we definitely always wanted the sweet stuff! My mom thought food was food and didn't question the ingredients or why the expiration period was longer than our ages combined. The older I got, the more food decisions I made for myself: pizza and Coke, the occasional McDonald's. I was a teen, and that's what everyone ate. In college and during my twenties, candy and Pizza Pockets were lifesavers!

As a money-conscious move, I would buy supersized packs of Kit Kat bars (because it was cheaper to get a pack of six than a single bar at the convenience store). After graduation I started my own graphic design business and it picked up very well, but it was difficult multitasking and staying on top of things. I would often work late, feel tired the next day, then pick myself up with caffeine and sugar. I started skipping meals and relied so much on sugar to keep me going that I carried a stash of sweets everywhere I went. I always had some chocolate bars or granola bars (because I thought they were healthier). I didn't have problems maintaining my weight and thought I was incredibly lucky that I could pig out and still fit into my jeans.

If I didn't have my sugar fix, you'd know it. My blood sugar highs and crashes meant I had uncontrollable mood swings and developed a short fuse. I was snappy and anxious throughout the day and had insomnia at night. I suffered from headaches and nagging cravings and often had "foggy brain" and could not concentrate.

It wasn't until years later that I looked back on this and started to connect the dots. My body was trying to tell me something. But I wasn't listening to my body—I was listening to my cravings. And after all, I still felt healthy and happy. A lot of my friends were complaining about stress, too, and I thought it was just normal, much like I thought it normal to meet a friend at Starbucks for a Caramel Frappuccino with whipped cream on top (which I now know means slurping 80 grams of sugar in minutes!). I exercised regularly, did yoga, and found downtime for relaxation and fun. I got married, I was building my dream career, we traveled, we bought our first house, I gave birth to a beautiful baby girl: Life was amazing!

Yet, only months later, I was in deep depression and losing control of my own body. I started developing mysterious symptoms. I had difficulty breathing and started gasping for air. I had difficulty chewing foods and swallowing. My limbs started to get weak. One day, as I was lifting my infant daughter out of her crib, my legs went so weak that I fell to the floor with her in my arms. She landed on my chest and was unhurt, but my head was bleeding. That began the scariest time of my life—not being able to trust my own body, not being able to hold my own baby.

Soon, I couldn't manage simple tasks that people take for granted, like brushing my hair, holding soap, walking, and getting up from a seated position. I even physically had trouble smiling. Yet I still kept working (I had no maternity leave). Medical tests all came back fine. According to my doctor, I was physically healthy and it was all in my head. My weakness and symptoms were overlooked, and I was diagnosed with postpartum depression.

I can't even count the many different antidepressants I was put on, and I still wasn't getting better. My depression even brought on suicidal symptoms—very far from the dreams I had of being a new mom. It wasn't until sixteen long months later that I was finally properly diagnosed—with myasthenia gravis, a rare neuromuscular autoimmune illness. The name *myasthenia gravis* literally translates from Latin as "grave muscle weakness" and is a chronic autoimmune neuromuscular disease characterized by varying degrees of weakness of the skeletal (voluntary) muscles of the body. MG medically has no cure. The treatments are surgery, immunosuppressants, and steroids that I didn't feel comfortable taking and to which my body didn't respond well.

But then it just hit me. It took one moment of clarity during one of my many crying-into-my-pillow episodes. That same voice that kept

saying, "Why me?" for months finally said, "I don't want to live like this!" In that moment, I believed in myself and realized it was up to *me* to change my life. I started to feel hopeful, and my inner voice started to become more positive and supportive.

I am so thankful we live in the times of the Internet. I googled everything I could think of about health and natural healing. I wanted to understand what the immune system was. I learned about candida and leaky gut syndrome, and about nutritional information for various foods and how they benefit healing.

I looked at what I was and wasn't eating and the possible missing nutrients in my diet, and I started to understand the food-health connection. That's when the question of how much sugar I was eating finally came up. I had a hunch that sugar was ruining my health and life, but I was reluctant to cut it out. So my first step was a sugar detox. I had to face the demon head-on. This very drastic move was frightening, but also empowering. After I cut out sugar, I continued eliminating other culprits, and within weeks I was off not only sugar but also wheat, gluten, dairy, and eggs.

Well, it wasn't as easy as that sounds. I fell off the wagon lots of times. My family's cooking had revolved around wheat, meat, eggs, and dairy—and of course sugar was everywhere. At first, I had no idea what I was going to eat after I eliminated all those things! The thought of removing something that I loved to eat scared me. But I felt that there was nothing else I could do but try. I could just try and see if it would help me or continue suffering and never be that happy mom my daughter deserved who could lift her onto the swing. It came down to a choice: whether or not *I* wanted to change.

I experimented in the kitchen and tried many new ingredients and recipes and had many complete fails. I practically had to relearn everything I knew about eating. But slowly my health started to improve and I started embracing this new way of eating. Saying no to certain foods didn't mean I was depriving myself but rather that I was making better, more nourishing food choices. I even enjoyed desserts again, and the sweet treats I was now eating were made with amazing-quality ingredients. And, best of all, I didn't feel sick or guilty after having a treat. Now I can happily say that my life is back to normal. I can hold both my daughters in my arms without worry, and our favorite activity is hitting the swings at our local playground.

These days, I see my health crisis as a blessing in disguise. It opened up a whole new wonderful world of healthier, unprocessed, organic, plant-empowered foods. And it introduced me to an online community of uplifting, inspiring, like-minded people whom I still treasure so much. I originally started blogging as an outlet for my depression, sharing my crafts and lifestyle photography to distract myself from my illness and struggles. When I rebranded my blog *Pure Ella* in 2012 and focused it on healthy cooking for gluten-free and plant-based recipes, it finally felt like all my skills, talents, and passions were under one roof. The blog began gaining popularity, and I received encouraging e-mails about how my lovely readers enjoyed my recipes and were inspired to make better health changes. And those e-mails and comments in turn inspired me to write this book.

The recipes here are all plant-based and gluten-free, but this book is for everyone, of all diet preferences. Plant-based recipes are neutral ground, since vegetarians, pescatarians, and meat eaters alike can always add any other foods on the side, as they wish. I think we can all agree that plant food is healthy, but it's not about becoming vegan or eating gluten-free. You can be vegan and/or gluten-free and still eat very unhealthy foods! My own diet changed for health reasons, but I am also happy to support sustainable farming practices, as well as limiting animal protein and looking to plant foods as our major nourishment source.

Most of all, these recipes are all free of refined sugar. My focus is on fresh vegetables and fruits, healthy fats, healthy proteins, and low-glycemic whole grains and carbohydrates. Most of all, these recipes are all free of refined sugar and use the best natural sweeteners that are more nourishing to your health.

I named my blog *Pure Ella* because to me, the most nourishing foods are pure: That means organic, unprocessed, with no refined sugars, or artificial coloring, or flavoring, or fillers—just as nature intended and definitely not made in a lab. I also believe in science and modern technology that can process amazing nutritional foods naturally and take them to the next level. For example, spirulina powder, protein powders, extracts of amazing natural foods like stevia or hydroponic gardens—foods that are fully natural and made easily accessible thanks to technology. I don't think we should eat like cavemen. Today nature can meet technology and be put to good use. (Sadly it is also used for GMOs—genetically modified foods—which I am not a proponent of.) Natural and organic foods are very important to me.

My food philosophy is about enjoying delicious, nourishing foods and not feeling deprived. Experiencing the power of nourishing food firsthand is so inspiring. When you eat well, you feel well. Simple as that. That's my goal: to help everyone live healthier and happier through foods that are good for you and taste great. More important, my view on healthy eating is to listen to your body. What works for you may not work for others. So it's important to look out for signals from your body. Learning to be more mindful of what you eat will change your relationship with food. *And that is sweet, indeed!*

—Ella

Sweet foods can be nourishing, interestingly enough, just not the sweets we often gravitate to. But you can change your relationship with food! You can make better food choices and enjoy better-for-you sweets to live healthier and happier.

INTRODUCTION

Let's Talk About Sugar, Sugar!

When we taste something sweet, our brain releases endorphins and serotonin, natural chemicals and hormones that pick up our mood, make us feel good, and even reduce stress and depression. Even breast milk is naturally sweet. It is simply human nature to enjoy sweets! I wrote this book to say that sweet foods can not only be enjoyable, they can be *nourishing*. The key is to make better choices and eat healthier sweets in moderation.

My approach is to *cut* the sugar, not *quit* it! The recipes in this book do this by replacing refined sugar with higher quality, natural, more nutritious sweeteners, and reducing the overall quantity of sweetener.

But when we look at the big picture, we can't just reduce the amount of sugar we consume. What we eat aside from sugar is just as important, so we don't feel deprived.

Cutting Out Sugar Is a Piece of Cake! (So to Speak)

If you simply *must* eat something sweet, try the following:

- Eat whole fruit.
- Eat a couple of dark chocolate squares (72 percent).
- Eat sweets alongside nuts and seeds, which both contain protein and fat.
- Make it an occasion. Fix tea, sit down, and relax; don't chow down a candy bar in the closet in thirty seconds.

- Make a healthy homemade treat from this book. (My go-to quick treat is the Healthy Three-Ingredient Chocolate Pudding, page 182.)

Eight Steps to Cut the Sugar

1. Purge and Prep

- Go through your whole kitchen and get rid of all sugary items.
- When grocery shopping, keep a list of healthy foods and stick to the list. Check for hidden and artificial sweeteners, and do not buy them. Avoid juice, "healthy" granola bars, processed foods, and "healthy" sweeteners.

2. Hydrate

- Drink more water! Water helps to clean out your body and satisfy cravings, even sweet ones.
- Lemon water especially cuts sweet cravings and alkalizes the body.
- Make your own fruity drinks! Choose low-glycemic fruit and add them to your water for simple Fruit-Infused Water (page 199).
- Drink unsweetened tea or coffee and enjoy their natural taste. Herbal and green teas are my favorites.

3. Don't Skip Meals

- If you don't eat regularly, you're more likely to binge and overeat next time.
- Meals should include healthy proteins and fats, vegetables, and whole low-glycemic grains such as quinoa or buckwheat.
- Between meals, snack on a handful of nuts and seeds if you feel hungry or experience sweet cravings.

4. Eat Healthy Fat

- Include healthy fats with every meal—they help our body absorb and assimilate the nutrients and help to improve our brain health.
- Drizzle baked and steamed foods with cold unrefined oils such as extra-virgin olive oil, pumpkin oil, and flax oil.
- Add coconut oil to oatmeal and porridge, or even coffee and tea.
- Add healthy oils such as coconut oil and flax oil to smoothies.
- Eat avocados.

5. Eat Healthy Protein

Proteins are essential building blocks for bones, muscles, cartilage, skin, and blood, as well as enzymes, hormones, and vitamins. Protein also makes you feel fuller longer and reduces your craving for sweets. It's easy to include healthy protein in every meal:

- Add sunflower, pumpkin, and chia seeds to oatmeal, smoothies, and salads.
- Eat beans and legumes such as lentils, adzuki beans, chickpeas, and black beans.
- Eat high-protein whole grains such as quinoa, buckwheat, amaranth, wild rice, and brown rice.

6. Eat Fruit

- Choose whole fruit when sugar cravings hit.
- Take fruit with you for a convenient, healthy snack food.
- Keep green apples and cut-up watermelon in the fridge as easy-to-grab snacks.

7. Trick Your Taste Buds

- Add spices such as cinnamon, ginger, nutmeg, or ground cloves to your tea or coffee, or to your morning porridge and snacks throughout the day.
- Add savory spices such as turmeric, curry, and cardamom, as well as fresh herbs such as mint, parsley, and cilantro to give your meals full flavor.
- Enjoy vegetables such as sweet potatoes, carrots, and cherry tomatoes, which contain small amounts of natural sugars.
- Develop a taste for bitter foods like radishes, arugula, or radicchio.

8. Distract Yourself!

Sugar will be calling your name, and you need fun ways to stop thinking about it. I like to go for a brisk walk and get some fresh air with lemon water by my side. Here are some other suggestions to get you through:

- Turn up the music and dance.
- Do yoga.
- Meditate.
- Brush your teeth.

Cut the Sugar Pantry

The secret to making great food is, of course, to use great ingredients. I have a well-stocked pantry and freezer, which makes shopping feel like less of a chore. I buy fresh produce weekly, and there's plenty to eat and get creative with. Convenience is so important to me now that I'm a busy mom. I want to create something delicious for my family without feeling stressed or spending hours in the kitchen.

These are some of my favorite foods I like to keep in regular stock. I look for whole foods that are unprocessed and free of any artificial additives such as colors and flavors. It's also important to look for organic, non-GMO foods, especially if you live in North America, and of course, watch out for hidden sugars.

Superfoods

"Superfoods" have more concentrated nutrition or unique health properties. Some of my favorite superfoods include the following:

Cinnamon. Sugar and spice is nice . . . especially when it comes to sugar and cinnamon. There are amazing properties in cinnamon that reduce blood sugar levels by decreasing the amount of glucose that enters the bloodstream after a meal. Cinnamon may also cut the risk of heart disease as it reduces the levels of total cholesterol, LDL cholesterol, and triglycerides, and increases HDL, the good cholesterol. Cinnamon is also loaded with powerful antioxidants, has anti-inflammatory properties, and helps fight bacterial and fungal infections. Incorporate it into your diet every day. I like it sprinkled in black tea or oatmeal, and in cacao-based smoothies. My daughter loves to dip apple slices in cinnamon. Look for Ceylon cinnamon; if it's not labeled "Ceylon," it will most likely be the Cassia variety. This variety is high in a naturally toxic compound called coumarin, and it's not advised to be eaten in quantities of over 1 teaspoon daily.

Chia Seeds. These tiny seeds are loaded with iron, calcium, magnesium, fiber, and omega-3 essential fatty acids, as well as providing a complete protein (2 tablespoons have 4 grams of protein). I love to add it to oatmeal, smoothies, and desserts for extra nutrition. For best results, chia seeds should be soaked or eaten with plenty of water because they are highly absorbent. Many recipes in this book make use of these powerful superseeds.

Flax seeds. One of the world's oldest fiber crops, flax seeds are a rich source of micronutrients, fiber, vitamin B_1, manganese, and omega-3 essential fatty acids. Regular flax seed consumption can even lower the risk of diabetes, cancer, and heart disease. Flax seeds should be ground for better absorption.

Hemp Seeds and Hemp Hearts. Rich in omega-3 fatty acids, calcium, and complete protein (3 tablespoons of hemp hearts provide 10 grams of protein), hemp seeds are fantastic to add in oatmeal, smoothies, baked goods, and savory dishes.

Maca. This earthy-tasting powder adds nutrition and boosts energy, memory, mental clarity, and even libido. Note that maca is not recommended for children.

Cacao Powder and Raw Cacao Nibs. The stuff chocolate is made of is actually incredibly healthy. Cacao powder and raw cacao nibs are rich in antioxidants, magnesium, calcium, zinc, iron, potassium, and more. They also affect certain neurotransmitters and trigger feel-good chemicals in the brain, decreasing depression and boosting energy. No wonder eating chocolate makes you happy! When choosing chocolate, look for fair-trade, dark, 70 percent or higher cacao content.

Goji Berries. Goji berries are a delicious dried fruit nutrient-rich in antioxidants and beta carotene. They are great for snacking as part of a trail mix or adding to recipes because they are naturally sweet and contain so much nutrition. A handful of goji berries (¼ cup) has 12 grams of sugar but also vitamin A, vitamin C, calcium, and iron.

Turmeric. This ancient Indian spice reduces inflammation and is high in antioxidants. Turmeric also boosts memory and overall brain health and lowers risk of illnesses such as depression, Alzheimer's disease, heart disease, cancer, and arthritis. Consuming black pepper with turmeric enhances the absorption of curcumin by 200 percent; otherwise it is poorly absorbed. I am constantly finding new ways of using this incredible spice, such as in my crackers (page 169), roasted chickpeas (page 36), and savory granola (page 34).

Himalayan Salt or Sea Salt. Salt has a bad reputation (and that still holds true for table salt, which is 97.5 percent sodium chloride), but mineral salts are very good for you, especially when we discuss sugar because a low-salt diet actually increases insulin resistance. Himalayan salt regulates the water content in the body, promotes healthy pH balance in cells, and reduces signs of aging. Pure sea salt also promotes a strong immune system, is alkalizing to the body, and helps food digest faster. Additionally, sea salt helps to reduce high cholesterol levels and maintain proper sugar levels in the body.

Nutritional Yeast. This superfood is worth finding and stocking. It is naturally rich in protein as well as vitamin B_{12} and other nutrients, and also lends a great cheesy flavor in recipes, such as the Cashew Cheese Ball (page 186) and Raw Cheesy Kale Chips (page 160). It keeps well if properly sealed and kept dry.

Seaweed. Sea vegetables are incredible sources of nutrition. They are blood purifying, high in calcium, alkalizing, antioxidant rich, detoxifying, and high in iodine for thyroid gland health and metabolism health. There are lots to choose from: nori (most commonly found in sushi rolls), kelp, dulse, arame, wakame, and kombu. All of these provide similar nutrition and different textures and colors, and work for different dishes. Try them and see what you like.

Grains and Grainlike Seeds

Grains have a mixed reputation right now, but not all grains are created equal. In fact, most of my carbohydrate intake is comprised of grainlike seeds, which are not only gluten free and highly nutritious, but much easier to digest. I choose low-glycemic grains as often as possible.

- **Quinoa**—Everybody's favorite gluten-free "grain" delivers complete protein, calcium, phosphorus, potassium, and iron. When I first introduced it to my family, I cooked quinoa half and half with rice so they could slowly get used to the flavor.

- **Millet**—Millet is very versatile, with a mellow, slightly sweet, nutty flavor. It is virtually nonallergenic and one of the few grains that is alkalizing to the body. Millet is considered a "smart carb" due to its high fiber and low glycemic index. It also acts as a prebiotic, feeding the microflora in your inner ecosystem. I like to use it in porridge, breakfast cake, soups or salads, or anywhere else I would use quinoa.

- **Buckwheat**—Though the name would make you think otherwise, buckwheat is another grainlike seed and unrelated to wheat. Buckwheat is a staple at our house because of my eastern European upbringing. It is high in

easily digestible proteins and has a low glycemic index—great for avoiding blood sugar crashes. Buckwheat can be found in three types: roasted, which has an earthy taste that is great in savory, hearty meals; unroasted, which has a light, more versatile flavor that is great in porridge; and raw, which blends well into raw desserts or granolas.

- **Amaranth**—This cousin of quinoa is also a great source of protein, calcium, magnesium, iron, and fiber.

- **Wild Rice**—I love the versatility, heartiness, nutrition, and great taste of wild rice, which is also misnamed. Wild rice is not a rice at all, but a seed high in protein, fiber, iron, B vitamins, folate, zinc, and magnesium. I love using it where I would normally use white rice, and I also enjoy mixing it into recipes such as Wild Rice Veggie Balls (page 75).

- **Brown Rice**—Brown rice is much lower in glycemic value than white rice, and it makes you feel fuller longer, has more fiber, and is overall more nutritious. I love it also because it's versatile in so many dishes, from salads to mains.

- **Oats**—Oats are probably the grain I cook with most, from oatmeal and overnight oats (page 5) for breakfast, to desserts and snacks such as Superhero Bars (page 167) and Mixed Berry Crumble Pots (page 108). One cup of cooked steel-cut oats has 10 grams of protein, making it a great breakfast. Steel-cut also has a lower glycemic value than instant oats. Oats are high in magnesium, iron, and fiber. Like all the grains discussed here, oats are naturally gluten free, but they can get contaminated in production. If you're gluten sensitive or have celiac disease, look for gluten-free certified brands.

Healthy Fats

These are some of the healthy fats that I keep in my pantry (aside from avocados).

- Coconut oil is the oil I cook and bake with the most. Coconut oil can also tolerate high-heat frying. I also love adding it to dessert recipes.
- Cold-pressed extra-virgin olive oil is the oil I use for salad dressings. It is a delicate oil that will turn to trans fat when overheated, so it's best to use cold. I drizzle it on top of pasta, rice, and quinoa once these are done cooking and toss to coat all over. This prevents them from sticking and adds the health benefits to our everyday meals.
- Grapeseed oil is my go-to oil for everyday use. It is mild in flavor so it doesn't take over my savory dishes. It tolerates only medium heat, so you still need to be careful to not overheat this oil when cooking.
- I occasionally splurge on other great healthy oils such as pumpkin oil, walnut oil, sesame seed oil, and avocado oil. These oils have amazing health benefits and I rotate them in my fridge (not pantry). Good quality oils should be kept in a cold dark area and refrigerated after opened because they go rancid quickly.

Nuts and Seeds (Also Healthy Fats)

We keep a huge variety of nuts and seeds on hand at all times. In addition to snacking on them often, I incorporate nuts and seeds into our meals and desserts, as you will see in many of the recipes in this book. Nuts and seeds have a high protein content and contain minerals such as manganese, magnesium, selenium, and potassium. For best absorption, you should soak nuts and seeds at least two to four hours before eating. It's best to keep your seeds and nuts refrigerated or keep small quantities in sealed glass jars because they do lose freshness within a few weeks.

My favorites include chia seeds, hemp hearts, flax seeds, pumpkin seeds, sunflower seeds, sesame seeds, cashews, Brazil nuts, almonds, walnuts, pecans, and pine nuts.

Beans and Lentils (Healthy Proteins)

Beans and lentils are an important part of my diet. They are an incredibly healthy source of protein (usually around 15 grams of protein per cup), iron, fiber, and so much more goodness. They are great for weight control and keep your heart healthy. Beans and lentils are also inexpensive and have a

long shelf-life (in dried form and in BPA-free cans), making them convenient as well. This means I stock up once for a few months.

Lentils. There are a few varieties, mostly referred to by their color: brown, green, red/yellow, and specialty. Whole lentils cook longer and split lentils cook much faster. I usually have both types on hand depending how quickly I want my dinner turned around.

Broad Beans/Fava Beans. I buy these frozen, and they literally cook in under five minutes. They're great for a quick salad or snack. My kids love them because they are soft and have a mild taste.

Chickpeas. These need no introduction. They are so delicious and versatile. I have plenty of recipes to prove this point, from my Wildly Delicious Roasted Chickpeas (page 36) to my Sweet & Spicy Chickpea Curry (page 101). And can you guess what puts the protein in my Protein Chocolate Chip Cookies (page 125)?

Other beans that are great to have are black beans, adzuki beans, and mung beans.

HOW TO SOAK & SPROUT BEANS, LENTILS & SEEDS

The following are the best ways to prep beans and lentils before cooking:

- **Soaking** — It's important to soak dry beans for eight to ten hours to remove naturally occurring toxins that interfere with proper digestion.
- **Sprouting** — Sprouting boosts the nutrition of beans, lentils, and seeds by 200 percent, so you get big return on your investment. Sprouted beans and lentils also purify the blood by adding oxygen to the blood during digestion.

You can sprout beans and lentils at home very easily without any special equipment. Simply soak a handful of dry beans or whole lentils (my favorites for this are adzuki and mung beans) in a jar overnight. Then rinse and strain over a plastic sieve (avoid metal). Leave on the sieve for the rest of the day in indirect sunlight. Rinse again (and toss) and place in the refrigerator overnight. Keep doing this for three to five days depending on the bean or lentil type until little sprouts appear. Add the sprouts to salads and sandwiches or just snack on them for a nutrition and protein boost.

Other Protein Sources

Soy Products. Tofu is a great protein source made from soy beans. It's important to buy organic tofu because soy is one of the top GMO crops. Too much soy can mess with your estrogen and thyroid levels, but you would need to consume high quantities daily to make it disrupt your hormones. We get a package of tofu once or twice a month, and when we have tofu we avoid soy milk. In moderation, it's a great neutral-tasting food source especially for its high-protein content. It's inexpensive and very versatile. You must try my Herbed Tofu-Stuffed Mini Peppers (page 78) and Parsley & Green Pea Savory Pancakes (page 22).

Edamame and soy milk are other sources of soy-derived protein. I love to rotate them so we don't consume them at the same time. I buy frozen non-GMO edamame beans and use them for salads and other dishes. They are also a good protein-rich snack for school lunches and family day trips. I usually get small snack-size packages of soy milk and keep them for days we're out at the park or traveling. They keep us hydrated and fueled with protein.

Protein Powders. These are great to have on hand. Protein smoothies are quick to make and can replace a meal in an emergency situation. Once you add some greens and a serving of fruit, they become such a great and convenient way to fuel up! There are a few great organic brands I love. Try a few different ones to find the flavor you really enjoy. I think the best are brown rice and pea combination powders—together they complete the amino acids and offer a complete protein. Avoid powders that have artificial sweeteners; look for ones with natural low-calorie sweeteners instead, such as stevia.

Plant Milks. Dairy is linked to so many health problems, so cutting it down or eliminating it for a month may be a great thing. It definitely helped me with my health, skin, bloating, sinusitis, and so much more. Ditching dairy will make room for healthier nutrient-packed foods and you'll feel light and energized after meals.

It's so easy to find dairy-free milk that the switch is super easy! The variety is endless, and different plant milks offer different benefits. Rotating them is a great thing to do. For example, soy milk is rich in protein, whereas other milks are not. Coconut milk is missing calcium (unless fortified). Hemp milk has omega-3 fats and 10 amino acids, but has a strong taste.

We use almond milk the most, and it's also the easiest to find, which is why I usually specify it in my recipes. But for the most part, plant milks are interchangeable, so use the one you like (except rice milk, which is too watery).

Look for organic, unsweetened, and carrageenan-free varieties, and watch out for added sugars (often listed as "evaporated cane juice"). Manufacturers add sugar to improve palatability of most plant milks. Look for unsweetened ones, or be mindful of the sugar grams so you don't go over 15 grams of sugar per serving.

HOW TO MAKE YOUR OWN NUT & SEED MILK

It's easy to make your own nut or seed milk. You'll need a high-speed blender and a cheesecloth or nut bag.

1 cup raw nuts, grains, or seeds of your choice

4 cups filtered water

1 to 2 pitted dates, for a little sweetness (optional)

1 teaspoon vanilla extract (optional)

Soak the nuts, grains, or seeds overnight in water. Rinse and strain. Place them in a blender with the water and blend on high until the mixture is smooth. Pour the mixture onto a cheesecloth-covered colander or a special nut bag. Squeeze to get most of the liquid out and pour the mixture back into the blender. Add the dates and vanilla extract, if using, to the blender. Blend again until smooth and serve. Reserve the pulp and add to oatmeal, smoothies, or baked goods. Fresh-made nut milk keeps for three to four days in a glass bottle or Mason jar in the refrigerator. Another benefit of making your own nut milk is that you can mix your favorite blend of nuts, oats, and seeds for your own delicious and healthy plant milk.

Here are my tips for successful gluten-free baking and some great natural egg replacers.

Baking

Gluten-Free Baking. When I first started to change my diet to gluten free, I had a hard time finding gluten-free flour mixes. I actually had to make my own from scratch. This was cumbersome at first, but thanks to trial and error, I began to understand gluten-free ingredients better and built my confidence in gluten-free baking. Now specialty ingredients are easier to find, which makes life a lot easier.

Oat Flour. This is one of my favorite flours because it has a very neutral taste. Be sure to get certified gluten-free oat flour if avoiding gluten is important to you.

Almond Flour. Almond flour is just ground-up blanched almonds, and you can even grind your own if you have a high-speed blender. It can be a pricey ingredient but so worth it—it makes your desserts nutrient- and protein-rich. Try my Chocolate-Dipped Almond & Cacao Nib Biscotti (page 128) to see what I mean!

Starches. These help ingredients bind together. Most starches are interchangeable, so you can use whichever you like: potato starch, arrowroot powder, or tapioca starch.

Gluten-Free All-Purpose Flour. I used store-bought mixes in these recipes to ensure readers will get the same results. (The one I use most often is Bob's Red Mill.) Other gluten-free flours that I like mixing into baking are: millet, sorghum, buckwheat, and

coconut. However, if you're keen on making your own, here is my tried-and-true recipe.

Wheat-Free Flours. There are lots of great flours that are glutinous and still more nutritious than wheat flour, if you're not concerned about gluten. My favorites are rye and spelt flour. Light spelt flour is light tasting and doesn't overpower most recipes, even desserts. Whole spelt flour is best for savory recipes such as the Black Bean–Tomato Tart (page 82).

Egg Replacers. With allergies on the rise, it's good to know a few tricks to bake egg free and dairy free, especially when the trick uses superfoods for added nutrition or is as simple as using applesauce!

- *Chia or flax egg*—Mix chia seeds or ground flax seeds with 1 to 3 tablespoons water in a small bowl and allow to stand for a few minutes. You can interchange chia seeds or ground flax seeds (and sometimes psyllium husk, such as in my Multiseed Bread, page 172).

Applesauce. I love using applesauce in my baked goods to replace eggs. The results are always amazing. Use unsweetened applesauce, or better yet make your own (page 171).

Bananas. You can also use ripe bananas in chewy baked goods or pancakes (page 12) to bind the ingredients together. Use 1 banana for 1 egg. However, be mindful of the high amount of sugar in bananas and reduce the total intake of sugar to a little to accommodate the extra sweetness.

ELLA'S GLUTEN-FREE ALL-PURPOSE FLOUR MIX

2 cups brown rice flour

2 cups sorghum flour

1 cup potato starch

1 cup arrowroot or tapioca powder

1 tablespoon chia powder (optional)

Whisk all the ingredients in a large bowl and transfer to a resealable container. If you're baking egg free, the chia powder helps to bind the ingredients together better. (If you can't find chia powder, you can grind chia seeds in a coffee grinder.)

BEST SUGAR SUBSTITUTES & NATURAL SWEETENERS

	Stevia	Rice Malt Syrup	Coconut Palm Sugar/ Coconut Nectar	Dates/Date Sugar/ Date Syrup	Raw Honey
Glycemic Index	0 (low GI)	25 (low GI)	35 (low GI)	42 (low GI)	55 (high GI)
Fructose	None	None	Low	Medium	Medium
Source	Derived from the stevia plant. Available as extract, sugar, and green powder.	Made from fermented cooked brown rice	Made from boiled and dehydrated sap of the coconut palm	Dried Medjool dates blend in well into desserts. Date sugar is ground-up dried dates	Made by honeybees from nectar (nonvegan), used since ancient times
Flavor	30% sweeter than sugar. Can have an aftertaste.	Mild tasting, low in sweetness	Has a rich depth of flavor	Rich and fudgy	Blends well into most recipes
Benefits	Has 0 sugar calories. Does not raise blood sugar.	No significant nutrition	Rich in vitamins and minerals, phytonutrients, and antioxidants	Loaded with vitamins and minerals such as magnesium and fiber	Rich in flavonoids, antioxidants, and antibacterial and antifungal properties
Bottom Line	Combine with natural sweeteners to diminish the aftertaste	Works in most recipes	Best for recipes with rich depth of either chocolate or spices	Date sugar doesn't fully melt so it's not suitable for all recipes.	Mild tasting. Great for raw recipes. Raw, manuka and dark varieties are best.

	Xylitol	Yacon Syrup	Blackstrap Molasses	Maple Syrup	Raw Cane Sugar/Sucanat/ Demerara
Glycemic Index	0 (low GI)	1-5 (low GI)	54 (med GI)	54 (med GI)	55 (high GI)
Fructose	None	None	Low	Medium	High
Source	Mainly derived from birch tree fibers. Considered a "sugar alcohol."	Made from yacon tubers (similar to potatoes)	The by-product of white sugar production; exceptional nutrition	Made from the sap of maple trees and minimally processed	Made from sugar cane but contains natural nutrients not stripped away as in white sugar
Flavor	Very similar to sugar. A bit bitter when heated.	Similar to raisin flavor with molasses	Very rich caramel-like flavor	Rich but neutral flavor	Most neutral tasting and most versatile
Benefits	Very low in calories. Does not raise blood sugar. No significant nutrition.	Increases energy levels, high in fiber, suppresses appetite	Very high in absorbable calcium, magnesium, and iron	Contains minerals and vitamins such as calcium, potassium, iron, and zinc	Very minimal nutrients
Bottom Line	Can cause digestive issues so use sparingly. Combine with other sweeteners. Avoid heating.	Not suitable for kids or pregnant/ nursing women	Intense flavor doesn't work well in many recipes	Rich on its own but blends well into most recipes	Closest to white sugar, with some nutrition

XYLITOL

HONEY

MAPLE SYRUP

STEVIA

RICE MALT SYRUP

RAW CANE SUGAR

DEMERARA SUGAR

COCONUT PALM SUGAR

DATE SUGAR

DATES

1 tbsp / 15 ml

1 tsp / 5 ml

Breakfast

Apple-Sweetened Oat Porridge

Serves 1

Oat porridge is a classic breakfast that is so comforting, filling, nutritious, and just hits the spot every time. You can change up the toppings and it's always a new bowl of goodness right in front of you. Oats are naturally very high in protein, and when you add superfoods like chia seeds and hemp seeds, it takes the nourishment to the next level. Blueberries and bananas are my favorite fruits because they are natural brain foods, and coconut oil melted into the oats adds healthy fats, which are also essential for brain health. Let's just say this is the perfect combination of foods to feel energized and fueled to start the day. Oats are naturally gluten-free, but if you are on a strict gluten-free regime, seek a certified gluten-free variety.

1 cup steel-cut oats

3 cups water

1 apple, diced

1 tablespoon coconut oil

To serve

½ cup almond milk per serving

½ ripe banana

handful of blueberries

1 tablespoon chia seeds

1 tablespoon hemp seeds

Bring the water to a boil in a medium pot. Add the apple (leaving the peel on is fine). Add the oats and stir to mix well. Lower the heat, cover, and simmer for about 5 minutes.

Remove from the heat and stir in the coconut oil. Scoop onto a bowl, pour the almond milk over the oatmeal, and top with the fruits and seeds.

BLUEBERRY & POMEGRANATE OVERNIGHT CHIA-OATS BREAKFAST PARFAITS

Serves 2

Overnight oats with chia seeds are life-changing! With a little planning the night before, and less than 5 minutes of prep, you can enjoy a great and healthy breakfast, leaving you with extra time to do great things . . . like morning yoga, perhaps? Prepping once to have breakfast done and waiting for three days is amazing. Have fun customizing these and mixing in different fruit or nuts and seeds.

½ cup oats (quick-cooking or rolled, and gluten-free if preferred)

2 tablespoons chia seeds

1 cup almond or hemp milk

1 ripe banana

¼ cup pomegranate arils

¼ cup fresh blueberries

1 to 2 teaspoons natural sweetener, such as honey or maple syrup, or 1 drop liquid stevia (optional)

The night before you plan to serve, mix the oats, chia seeds, and milk in an airtight container. Cover and place in the refrigerator overnight.

In the morning, slice the banana and layer the oat mixture and the fruits in a glass or a Mason jar.

NOTE Additional sweetener is not recommended if you will be adding fresh fruit, as you don't want your breakfast overly sweet. If you're used to sweet breakfasts, try adding about 1 teaspoon raw honey (or maple syrup for a vegan option) and then slowly reducing the amount over time. If you want a zero carbohydrate sweetener, stevia is a great choice to try.

French Crêpes

Serves 2 or 3

I grew up on crêpes. My mom made them for breakfast, lunch, and dinner—there were no rules for when and how we ate them. My favorite filling was jam, preferably homemade. I still love them so much and make a double batch on Sunday mornings. It's a tough job, because each one disappears from the plate instantly! Serve them warm with Vanilla-Cashew Cream Cheese and Raspberry-Chia Jam, topped with fresh raspberries and mint. Voilà! A stunning breakfast or dessert. If you're feeding a family, it's great to have two pans going at once so you can cut the cooking time in half.

¾ cup sweet rice flour

½ cup coconut flour

3 tablespoons potato starch

1 tablespoon powdered stevia

1 tablespoon raw cane sugar

Pinch of fine sea salt

¼ cup coconut oil, melted, or grapeseed oil

½ cup almond milk

1¼ to 1½ cups water, warmed

Vanilla-Cashew Cream Cheese, for serving (recipe follows)

Raspberry Chia Jam, for serving (recipe follows)

NOTE The smaller and lighter the pan, the easier it is to work with. Keep the pan hot and oiled so that the crêpe won't stick. You need a good nonstick pan—cast-iron is great; stainless steel won't work as well.

In a medium bowl, sift together and whisk the flours, potato starch, stevia, sugar, and salt. Add the oil and milk and stir to combine. Pour in the water slowly while continuing to mix the batter. You're after a fairly pourable consistency in the batter, and you may need less or more of the water (I find that about 1¼ cups works great). If the batter seems clumpy, either press it against the side of the bowl with a wooden spoon to break the lumps, or use an immersion blender to get a smooth consistency.

Heat a small nonstick pan over medium-high heat with a little oil and pour in a ladleful of batter. Your pan and oil have to be hot or else the batter will stick and this will ruin the crêpe. Quickly grab the pan and swirl the batter inside so it spreads out to the sides. Set back down and cook for about 2 minutes, or until bubbles appear on top and the crêpe is slightly golden underneath (check by lifting an edge with a spatula). Gently flip the crêpe over and cook the other side for just another minute or two. Continue with all the batter.

Vanilla-Cashew Cream Cheese

Serves 2 or 3

1 cup raw cashews, soaked in water for at least 2 hours

½ cup vanilla dairy-free yogurt

½ teaspoon vanilla extract

3 Medjool dates, pitted, or 2 drops liquid stevia

Rinse and drain the cashews and place in a food processor. Grind them on high speed, and then add the rest of the ingredients and process until smooth. Transfer to a bowl, cover, and store in the refrigerator for up to 3 days.

Raspberry-Chia Jam

Makes 3 cups

3 cups fresh raspberries

2 tablespoons chia seeds, whole or ground

4 to 6 drops liquid stevia (optional)

Purée the raspberries in a blender. Transfer to a bowl, add the chia seeds and stevia and mix until well combined. Cover and refrigerate for 4 to 6 hours; overnight is even better, for the chia seeds to plump up and the texture to become thicker, resembling jam. Taste and sweeten with stevia if a little extra sweetness is preferred.

The sweetness level really depends on your taste preference—but it's worth considering that all fruits already have natural sugars. This jam will keep well in the fridge for up to 5 days (if it lasts that long). Frozen fruit could work well, too, especially in the winter months.

NOTE Frozen fruit could work well here, too, especially in the winter months. This will not keep well as a preserve or canned jam—it's meant to be eaten immediately!

CHIA WAFFLES

Serves 2 or 3

Waffles are my favorite! It's such a treat to serve these on Sunday mornings, fresh off the waffle iron with assorted toppings in bowls set on the table for easy custom-topped deliciousness. But dessert for breakfast is no longer my thing. And it shouldn't be yours, either. That's why I love reinventing recipes to make them healthier and better. These are not only gluten-free and vegan but also high in protein and chia goodness. I never thought waffles could be nourishing, but these pass the test. They're wholesome, delicious, and filling—no longer just empty carbs! Top with fresh fruit, puréed strawberry sauce, and whipped coconut.

2 tablespoons chia seeds, whole or ground

6 tablespoons water

1 cup oat flour*

½ cup sorghum flour*

¼ cup potato starch*

½ teaspoon baking powder

1 cup almond milk

2 tablespoons coconut oil, melted, or grapeseed oil, plus more for coating waffle iron

2 tablespoons coconut nectar or 2 drops liquid stevia

Whipped Coconut Milk

1 (14 ounces) can full-fat coconut milk, refrigerated

Stewed Strawberries (page 142), for serving

Fresh berries, for serving

*or substitute 1¾ cup all-purpose gluten-free flour for these 3

In a small bowl, mix the chia with the water and let sit for 5 to 10 minutes.

In a large bowl, whisk the flours, potato starch, and baking powder. Add the almond milk, oil, sweetener and the chia mixture and mix to combine well. Let rest for 10 to 20 minutes.

Heat a waffle iron and brush with oil. Scoop a ladleful of batter onto the waffle iron and bake per the manufacturer's instructions until golden brown.

To make the Whipped Coconut Milk, drain the coconut milk can of liquid and scoop the cream to a bowl. (The coconut water can be drunk or added to smoothies.) Whip with a mixer to make fluffy (or just scoop and serve).

Top the waffles with the Stewed Strawberries, Whipped Coconut Milk, and fresh berries.

BANANA-SWEETENED BLUEBERRY PROTEIN PANCAKES

Serves 2 or 3

We love pancakes at our house. Hearing my daughter Gabriella call out, "Mommy, can you make pancakes?" is music to my ears on the weekends. Of course I love making her happy, and blueberry pancakes are her favorite. I make up a jar of the dry ingredients and keep it handy, making life a little easier when there's a baby around.

2 tablespoons ground flax seeds

6 tablespoons water

1 cup all-purpose gluten-free flour or light spelt flour

2 tablespoons vanilla protein powder

2 teaspoons baking powder

¾ to 1 cup almond milk

1 ripe banana

1 cup fresh blueberries, plus more for serving

1 teaspoon coconut oil, melted

Rice malt or maple syrup, for serving

In a small bowl, mix the flax seeds with the water and set aside.

In another bowl, whisk the flours, protein powder, and baking powder. Add the almond milk and flax mix and combine well. Smash the banana with a fork and mix it into the batter and set aside for 10 minutes. Coat the blueberries with flour and stir them into the batter just before making the pancakes.

Heat a large cast-iron pan over medium-high heat with the coconut oil. Scoop 2 to 3 tablespoons of the batter into the pan per pancake and brown the pancakes on both sides.

 NOTE Top with rice malt syrup instead of maple syrup so it's lower in sugar, and avoid placing any syrups on the table for second helpings. This way you're not tempted to drench your pancakes with extra sugar.

MILLET-APPLE BREAKFAST CAKE

Serves 6 to 8

When millet was touted recently as a "super grain," I casually mentioned it to my mom and she laughed, saying we grew up on millet in Poland. She pulled many recipes for it straight from memory. Millet is an ancient grain that is incredibly healthy. It's also gluten-free, easy to digest, and great for those with food sensitivities. Millet is alkalizing to the body and acts as a prebiotic that helps feed good bacteria.

When I first started changing my diet, millet became a huge staple in my kitchen and still is today. This recipe is inspired by my mom's millet porridge with apples that she served us kids for breakfast. We loved it, and now it's great to see my own kids enjoy these simple ingredients in this delicious breakfast cake. It's delicious, simple, and a very healthy way to start the day.

1 cup millet

3 cups almond milk

2 teaspoons vanilla extract (optional)

4 medium apples, cored, peeled, and shredded (about 2 cups)

1 teaspoon ground cinnamon

¾ cup slivered or chopped raw almonds

In a medium saucepan, cook the millet in the almond milk over medium heat until soft, stirring occasionally, about 20 minutes. Turn off the heat and let stand covered for an additional 5 minutes to fully soften. Stir in the vanilla extract until well combined.

Preheat the oven to 350°F and grease an 8-inch pie or casserole dish.

Mix the shredded apples with the cooked millet and cinnamon and pour the mixture into the baking dish. Sprinkle the almonds on top and bake uncovered for 25 minutes or until almonds turn slightly golden. Remove from oven and allow to cool 10 minutes before serving. Keeps well for up to 5 days refrigerated. Makes great leftovers! This can be made ahead of time and reheated just before serving, to be eaten as slices or scooped into a bowl with warm almond milk.

Coconut & Goji Berry Granola & Bars

Serves 8 to 10

Making your own granola is so simple and so rewarding. I love it because I know what's in it and I can customize the recipe to my liking with every batch (you can too!). Store-bought granola is also loaded with sugar. Even when it's healthier kinds of sugar, it's always been too sweet for my liking.

A lot of recipes use sweeteners as the actual binder to make those little crunchy clusters. I like to use a combination of the nutritious chia and flax seeds as my "glue" to make those clusters stay together—perfect for the bowl with some warm almond milk, perfect for snacking, and perfect for granola bars, too. Yes, the same recipe makes granola bars for a great nutritious breakfast to go or midday snack!

¼ cup ground flax seeds

¼ cup chia seeds

5 drops liquid stevia

½ cup water

3 cups rolled oats

½ cup raw almonds, chopped

½ cup sunflower seeds

½ cup pumpkin seeds

¼ cup hemp heart seeds

3 tablespoons raw cacao nibs

6 tablespoons rice malt syrup or honey

¼ cup coconut oil, melted

½ cup unsweetened coconut flakes (reserve)

¼ cup goji berries (reserve)

Granola Bars

⅓ cup honey or maple syrup

GRANOLA

Preheat the oven to 350°F and line a baking sheet with parchment paper.

In a small bowl, mix the flax seeds, chia seeds, stevia, and water and set aside.

In a large bowl, combine the oats, almonds, sunflower seeds, pumpkin seeds, hemp seeds, and cacao nibs. Mix in the syrup and coconut oil and toss to incorporate well. Add in the flax-chia mixture and mix all the ingredients together well. Fold in the coconut flakes.

Spread the mixture evenly onto the baking sheet and bake for 20 to 30 minutes, flipping and tossing the granola halfway through the baking time to break it up.

Let cool, then mix in the goji berries. Store in a sealed Mason jar for up to 1 month. Enjoy with almond milk or as a topping to yogurt, chia pudding, or oatmeal.

Granola Bars

Preheat the oven to 250°F and line an 8-inch square baking pan with parchment paper. Prepare the Granola mixture on page 16, with the addition of the honey. Press it very firmly and evenly into the bottom of the pan. Bake for 45 to 50 minutes, until the top looks dry and is slightly golden. Transfer to a cooling rack and let cool completely. Slice into bars and enjoy. Wrap individual bars in parchment paper and store in an airtight container in the refrigerator for up to 3 weeks or at room temperature for up to 5 days. These also freeze well for a quick grab-and-go!

Avocado Toast

Serves 1

So simple and easy and yet life-changing. I like my slice of bread seedy and hearty with smashed avocado, tomato, sprouts, and a sprinkle of fine sea salt and cayenne pepper.

2 slices Multiseed Bread (page 172) or your favorite bread

1 ripe avocado

Sprinkle of Himalayan pink or sea salt

Pinch of cayenne pepper

4 tomato slices

Handful of your favorite sprouts

Toast the bread. Pit and peel the avocado and smash it onto each piece of toast. Sprinkle with salt and cayenne. Top with the tomatoes and sprouts.

DAIRY-FREE CREAM CHEESE

Serves 1

If you're living dairy-free or trying to eat less dairy, this is a delicious recipe for you to know by heart and make anytime, any day. It's quick and easy and really does have the taste and texture of cream cheese—yum! And it's a great source of protein. I recommend spreading it on gluten-free bagels or Multiseed Bread (page 172), with organic cucumber slices, cherry tomatoes, pea shoots or other sprouts, and extra chopped chives as toppings.

½ package firm tofu (¼ of 16 ounce package)

2 heaping tablespoons Vegenaise or other mayonnaise

1 teaspoon sweet paprika

½ to 1 teaspoon sea salt

Freshly ground black pepper

1 tablespoon finely chopped onion

1 tablespoon chopped fresh chives

Mix the tofu, mayonnaise, paprika, salt, and pepper to taste in a food processor until smooth. Alternatively, use an immersion blender or mix well with a fork until well combined.

Transfer to a bowl and fold in the onion and chives. Spread on bagels and toast for a protein-rich breakfast or lunch. Keeps for up to 3 days refrigerated.

Parsley & Green Pea Savory Pancakes

Serves 2 or 3

Savory pancakes put a new healthy twist on a classic breakfast. These are amazingly delicious with such bold, exciting flavors. They are great for breakfast or brunch but are even doable as a quick weeknight supper.

½ cup chickpea flour

½ cup water

½ cup firm tofu (¼ of 16-ounce package)

1 tablespoon nutritional yeast flakes

½ teaspoon paprika

½ teaspoon fine sea salt

¼ teaspoon freshly ground black pepper

½ teaspoon ground turmeric

½ teaspoon baking powder

½ cup peas, cooked and drained (fresh or frozen; I use frozen)

¼ cup chopped fresh flat-leaf parsley, plus more for serving

Grapeseed oil, for cooking

1 ripe avocado, for serving

Tahini Sauce (page 89), for serving

In a small bowl, combine the chickpea flour and water and set aside for 30 minutes (or place in the refrigerator overnight).

When ready to cook, put the tofu, yeast flakes, paprika, salt, pepper, turmeric, baking powder, and chickpea mixture in a food processor and mix until a smooth batter forms. Transfer the mixture to a bowl and mix in the peas and parsley.

Heat a large cast-iron pan over medium-high heat and drizzle in oil to coat the bottom of the pan. Scoop 2 to 3 tablespoons of the batter into the pan per pancake and cook until the tops turn dry and the bottom turns golden brown. Flip over with a spatula and cook until golden brown on the other side. Serve hot, sprinkled with the extra parsley, avocado, and Tahini Sauce.

Caramelized Onion, Leek & Potato Chickpea Frittata

Serves 4 to 6

I've always been an egg lover and loved making traditional frittatas! So I could not believe my excitement at making an egg-free frittata that was so incredibly tasty. Chickpea flour is magic. That's a fact. And this recipe is so versatile, as you can essentially change up the filling ingredients to your personal liking. I like using leftover cooked whole potatoes in this dish. The caramelized onions and leeks make it all so good. Try topping it off with fresh arugula for a nice peppery touch. We love some "free tata" or "free mama" on those lazy weekends. (Sorry for the inside jokes!)

¾ cup chickpea flour

1 cup water

½ cup firm tofu (¼ of 16-ounce package)

1 tablespoon nutritional yeast flakes

Grapeseed oil for cooking

1 medium sweet onion, diced

3 medium cooked potatoes, sliced (use leftover boiled potatoes)

1 leek, rinsed well and thinly sliced (reserve about ¼ cup for topping)

1 teaspoon fine sea salt

¼ teaspoon freshly ground black pepper

¼ teaspoon cayenne pepper

Scallions, chopped, for serving

Arugula, for serving

In a bowl, mix the chickpea flour with the water and set aside for about 30 minutes (or overnight in the refrigerator).

When ready to make the frittata, preheat the oven to 350°F.

Put the chickpea mixture, tofu, and yeast flakes in a food processor and mix until a smooth batter forms.

Heat a large cast-iron (ovenproof) skillet over medium-low heat, drizzle in some oil, and sauté the onions until golden. Add the potatoes and leeks and cook for about 5 minutes, or until softened. Pour the chickpea batter into the pan, stir, sprinkle with salt and peppers, and place in the oven.

Bake for 25 to 35 minutes, until the top is set. Serve hot with the extra leeks, the scallions, and the arugula.

CHICKPEA CRÊPES
WITH SMASHED CHICKPEA FILLING

Serves 4

Breakfast and chickpeas were always my favorite things, but I never imagined they could go together so well. You can make the crêpe batter the night before so it's ready in the morning. These crêpes are high in protein and so delicious, the best way to fuel you for the day. They make a great lunch, too.

Crêpes

1 cup water (+ ¼ extra)

1 cup chickpea flour

2 tablespoons nutritional yeast flakes

1 teaspoon fine sea salt

½ teaspoon ground turmeric

¼ teaspoon baking powder

Grapeseed oil, for cooking

Filling

2 cups canned chickpeas, rinsed and drained

¼ cup chopped onion

¼ cup chopped fresh flat-leaf parsley or cilantro

1 tablespoon freshly squeezed lemon juice

1 teaspoon mustard

1 teaspoon ground turmeric

½ teaspoon ground cumin

Freshly ground black pepper

3 tablespoons extra-virgin olive oil

Avocado, sliced, for serving

Arugula, for serving

Cherry tomatoes, sliced, for serving

Sprouts, for serving

For the crêpes: Mix all of the ingredients together in a food processor or using an immersion blender. Transfer to a bowl and set aside for 30 minutes (or refrigerate overnight).

For the filling: Place all of the ingredients in a food processor and mix until small, slightly sticky crumbs form. Transfer to a bowl.

To serve: Heat a small nonstick pan with grapeseed oil over medium-high heat. Scoop or pour about ¼ cup of batter into the pan and cook until bubbles form on top and the bottom is nice and golden. Flip over with a spatula and cook for another minute or two. Remove from the pan with a spatula and continue with all of the batter.

Fill the crêpes with the chickpea filling and fold over. Serve with the avocado, arugula, cherry tomatoes, and sprouts.

Salads & Appetizers

Massaged Kale Salad with Butternut Squash

Serves 1

I discovered kale along with blogging. And I have to admit, it was tough love from day one (with kale, not blogging). Despite the kale craze, I knew it was healthy, so I kept chugging it down like a good sport. It wasn't until I finally discovered the best way to eat fresh kale. Kale needs to be rubbed the right way—a little oil and muscle makes those tough leaves soft and more delicate and more delicious. This salad is lovely on a fall or winter day. I like it when the butternut squash is still warm from being roasted in the oven.

2 cups butternut squash, pre-cooked and cubed (great to use leftovers)

2 packed handfuls kale leaves (curly or dino is great, but any variety will do)

¼ cup olive oil

Juice of ½ lemon

¼ teaspoon sea salt

1 clove garlic, minced

2 tablespoons raw apple cider vinegar

2 teaspoons maple syrup (optional)

1 teaspoon Dijon mustard

Freshly ground black pepper

Superseed Savory Granola (page 34), for serving

Wildly Delicious Roasted Chickpeas (page 36), for serving

Preheat the oven to 350°F and line a baking sheet with parchment paper.

Cut the squash in half lengthwise, scoop out the seeds and strings, and place the halves face down on the baking sheet. Bake for about 45 minutes. Let cool, then peel the squash, and chop the flesh into chunks.

To make the salad, stem the kale leaves. Basically you're pulling the soft leafy parts off the stems with your fingers. Place the kale pieces in a large bowl and add the olive oil, lemon juice, and salt. Put your clean hands in there and give the leaves a good massage for about 5 minutes. The more massaging the kale gets, the softer the leaves become (and thus the more delicious).

Add the garlic, vinegar, maple syrup, mustard, and pepper to taste and toss. Top with the butternut squash chunks, the Superseed Savory Granola, and the Wildly Delicious Roasted Chickpeas.

Brussels Sprouts & Radish Spring Salad

Serves 1

One of my favorite salads with a spring note: The cabbage, brussels sprouts, and radishes make a stunning salad, and the dressing complements this wonderful burst of flavors.

2 or 3 kale leaves, stemmed and torn into small pieces

1 cup thinly shredded green cabbage

Handful of radicchio, thinly sliced

10 brussels sprouts, thinly sliced or shredded

6 radishes, thinly sliced

Maple-Mustard-Lemon Dressing, for serving (recipe follows)

Toss the kale, cabbage, radicchio, brussels sprouts, and radishes in a large bowl. Add the dressing and toss to combine.

Maple-Mustard-Lemon Dressing

Serves 1

¼ cup Vegenaise or other mayonnaise

Juice of ½ lemon

2 tablespoons olive oil

2 tablespoons maple syrup

1 heaping tablespoon grainy mustard

Sea salt and freshly ground black pepper

In a small bowl or Mason jar, whisk or shake all the ingredients until they emulsify. The dressing will keep in the refrigerator for up to 1 week.

Superseed Savory Granola

Serves 4 to 6

The crunchy texture of this granola and the exciting flavor combination make this granola ahhh-mazing! It's also such a versatile recipe as a topping for all sorts of dishes—salads and soups are my favorites. But it makes a pretty darn good snack just all on its own, too!

2 tablespoons ground flax seeds

¼ cup water, warmed

¼ cup pumpkin seeds

¼ cup sunflower seeds

¼ cup buckwheat groats

2 tablespoons hemp heart seeds

2 tablespoons maple syrup

½ teaspoon ground turmeric

¼ teaspoon spicy Hungarian paprika or chili powder

¼ teaspoon sea salt

¼ teaspoon freshly ground black pepper

Preheat the oven to 300°F and line a baking sheet with parchment paper.

In a small bowl, mix the flax seeds with the water and set aside for about 5 minutes.

Place all of the remaining ingredients in another bowl, add the flax mixture, and toss to combine well. Scoop onto the baking sheet and spread out evenly.

Bake for about 30 minutes, tossing the mixture halfway through the baking time to break it up. Allow to cool before removing from the baking sheet.

The granola will keep well in an airtight container for up to 1 week at room temperature or 3 weeks refrigerated.

WILDLY DELICIOUS ROASTED CHICKPEAS

Serves 4

Roasted chickpeas make a great add-in to salads and soups and they even make a great snack on their own. With the addition of spices such as turmeric, they really are wildly delicious!

2 tablespoons ground flax seeds

¼ cup warm water

1½ cups canned chickpeas, rinsed and drained

¼ cup olive oil

2 tablespoons maple syrup (optional)

½ teaspoon ground turmeric

½ teaspoon spicy Hungarian paprika or chili powder

½ teaspoon ground cumin

¼ teaspoon sea salt

¼ teaspoon freshly ground black pepper

Preheat the oven to 300°F and line a baking sheet with parchment paper.

In a small bowl, mix the flax seeds with the water and set aside for about 5 minutes.

Place all of the remaining ingredients in another bowl, add the flax mixture, and toss to combine well. Scoop onto the baking sheet and spread out evenly.

Bake for about 30 minutes, tossing the mixture halfway through the baking time to break it up. Allow to cool slightly before removing from the baking sheet.

CRISPY SWEET POTATO WEDGES

Serves 4

Sweet potatoes are healthier than white because they are lower on the glycemic scale and have more nutrition. We love them also because they are sweet and delicious. These crispy seasoned wedges are super tasty and just awesome! They make a great side dish, but they are also terrific on their own for snacking.

4 large sweet potatoes, peeled or not according to your preference

¼ cup olive oil

Sea salt and freshly cracked black pepper

1 cup Japanese-style rice crackers, natural flavor

Preheat the oven to 350°F and line a baking sheet with parchment paper and set aside. Cut the potatoes into wedges of equal size to bake evenly. Place in a large bowl, drizzle with 2 tablespoons of the olive oil, and season with salt and pepper to taste.

In a food processor, pulse the crackers until crumbs form. Some larger pieces are fine to leave for a bigger crunch! Alternatively, put the rice crackers in a plastic bag or between sheets of parchment paper and smash into crumbs with the back of a wooden spoon. Sprinkle the cracker crumbs on the wedges and toss to coat evenly.

Drizzle the baking dish with the remaining 2 tablespoons olive oil, and spread the sweet potato wedges evenly on the sheet. Bake for about 30 minutes, flipping once halfway through the baking time until the potatoes are soft and the crumbs are golden. Serve immediately.

PURE GODDESS SALAD

Serves 1

These are all my favorite ingredients in one delicious, filling, big salad. Kale, sprouts, quinoa, broccoli, crunchy nuts and seeds, with a little sweetness from pomegranate arils. And the dressing is a marriage between sweet, spicy, and tangy. Purely delicious.

½ cooked cup quinoa

Bunch of kale, stemmed and shredded

¼ cup extra-virgin olive oil

Juice of ½ lemon

1 cup chopped broccoli florets

⅛ medium red onion, finely chopped

½ cup cooked edamame beans

¼ cup raw pine nuts

¼ cup pumpkin seeds

¼ cup sunflower seeds

Pure Goddess Dressing (recipe follows)

Sprouts (use your favorite), for topping

Small handful of pomegranate arils, for topping

Cook the quinoa according to the package instructions. In a large bowl, massage the kale (as suggested on page 31) with the oil and lemon juice. Add the quinoa, broccoli, onion, edamame, pine nuts, and both seeds and toss to combine. Add the dressing and toss again. Top with sprouts and pomegranate arils and serve.

PURE GODDESS DRESSING

Serves 1

¼ cup extra-virgin olive oil

Juice of ½ lemon

2 tablespoons miso paste

2 tablespoons maple syrup

In a small bowl or Mason jar, place all of the ingredients and whisk or shake to combine. Drizzle over the Pure Goddess Salad or any favorite salad. Store sealed in the jar for up to 1 week.

Bittersweet Marinated Kale, Radicchio & Blackberry Salad

Serves 4

Opposites attract in this delicious salad. Bitters are so amazing for your digestive health—they really kick up your metabolism and curb cravings, too. Pairing them with a little sweetness, like these gorgeous blackberries, results in the perfect marriage of bitter and sweet.

Bunch of kale, stemmed

½ cup shredded red cabbage

¼ cup shredded radicchio

¼ small red onion or 3 shallots, thinly sliced

¼ cup pine nuts

¼ cup pumpkin seeds

½ cup edamame beans

½ cup chopped scallions

Sweet Dijon Dressing (recipe follows)

1 cup fresh blackberries (optional)

Lime wedges, for serving (optional)

Tear the kale into small pieces. (For best results, massage the kale as suggested on page 31). Transfer to a large bowl. Add the cabbage, radicchio, onion, pine nuts, pumpkin seeds, edamame, and scallions. Toss with the dressing and top with blackberries. Garnish with the lime wedges.

Sweet Dijon Dressing

Serves 4

¼ cup extra-virgin olive oil

2 tablespoons raw apple cider vinegar

2 tablespoons honey

1 teaspoon Dijon mustard

Pinch of sea salt

Freshly ground black pepper

In a small bowl or Mason jar, place all of the ingredients and whisk or shake to combine. Refrigerate in a glass jar for up to 3 days. Serve over your favorite salad.

Baby Spinach, Heirloom Tomato & Asparagus Salad

Serves 4

Asparagus is a thing of beauty. In this spring-style salad, the simple garden vegetables work so well together smothered with the ever-so-good-for-you hemp oil vinaigrette. A sprinkling of sprouts, in this case home-sprouted mung beans, boosts the protein and vitamin value in this salad and really takes it to new heights.

1 pound asparagus spears, tough ends removed

4 handfuls baby spinach

2 cups heirloom cherry tomatoes, halved

Handful of your favorite sprouts (see how to sprout your own, page xxi)

Hemp Oil Vinaigrette, for serving (recipe follows)

Steam the asparagus on the stovetop until cooked to your liking. Blanch in ice water after it's steamed, then strain on a colander.

On a platter, arrange a layer of spinach, and top with the tomatoes, cut up asparagus, and sprouts. Drizzle the dressing over the top and serve.

Hemp Oil Vinaigrette

Serves 4

¼ cup extra-virgin olive oil

2 tablespoons hemp oil

Juice of ½ lemon

1 teaspoon dried oregano

1 teaspoon dried basil

Sea salt and freshly ground black pepper

In a small bowl or Mason jar, place all of the ingredients and whisk or shake to combine. Season with the salt and pepper. Store sealed in the jar for up to 1 week in the fridge.

Raw Veggie Pâté

Serves 4 to 6

Vegetable pâté is my current obsession! There's so much goodness here with amazing healthy ingredients and exciting spices. This recipe is so versatile, too—it makes a great sandwich spread, raw pasta sauce, or delicious sauce for zucchini noodles. It also excites the simplest of dishes, like a simple salad. Sometimes you don't need much to make a delicious and fun dish.

1 cup raw sunflower seeds, soaked in water for at least 2 hours

1 celery stalk

1 medium carrot

½ medium onion

½ cup fresh flat-leaf parsley, chopped

Juice of ½ lemon

2 tablespoons olive oil

1 teaspoon celery seeds

1 teaspoon ground turmeric

½ to 1 teaspoon spicy Hungarian paprika

½ teaspoon freshly ground black pepper

½ teaspoon sea salt or more to taste

Rinse and drain the sunflower seeds, and pat dry with a paper towel. Place them in a food processor and grind until crumbs form. Add all of the remaining ingredients and process on high speed until a paste forms.

Great to serve with a salad or use as a sandwich spread or veggie dip. Store in a resealable glass container in the refrigerator for up to 5 days.

Watercress & Watermelon Radish Salad

Serves 1

Pure food is so naturally beautiful. I get excited when I see beauty in real, fresh vegetables and fruit. But my heart skipped a beat the first time I laid my eyes on watermelon radishes. Their natural beauty, color, texture, and flavor is a real work of art created by Mother Nature. In this salad, their beauty shines so bright and their flavor works so great with the peppery watercress and bright lemony dressing. Together these ingredients excite all your senses!

Bunch of watercress (3 or 4 handfuls)

¼ cup thinly sliced red onion

1 English cucumber, sliced

4 watermelon radishes, thinly sliced

Simple Lemon & Olive Oil Dressing, for serving (recipe follows)

Pick the stems off the watercress and place in bowls. Add the onion, cucumber, and radishes and toss. Drizzle the dressing on top, toss again, and serve.

Simple Lemon & Olive Oil Dressing

Serves 1

¼ cup olive oil

Juice of ½ lemon

Pinch of sea salt

Freshly ground black pepper to taste

Place all of the ingredients in a small bowl or Mason jar and whisk or shake until combined. Drizzle over the salad. Store in a resealable glass container in the refrigerator for up to 5 days.

Roasted Beets in Field Greens with Superfood Sprinkle

Serves 4

I've always loved beets. I have childhood memories of sneaking into our kitchen when my mom was cooking and picking freshly cooked, steamy beets off a plate. I remember burning my fingertips a few times. Years later, I still catch myself mesmerized by their sweet flavor and applaud my childhood sneakiness and bravery.

4 or 5 medium beets

Olive oil, for drizzling

4 handfuls mixed field greens or mesclun

3 shallots, chopped

½ cup Superfood Sprinkle (recipe follows)

Juice of ½ lemon

Sea salt and freshly ground black pepper

Preheat the oven to 350°F and line a baking sheet with parchment paper. Peel the beets, cut into wedges, and toss in olive oil. Place on the baking sheet and roast for 20 to 30 minutes. Put the greens in a large bowl and top with the beets (still warm is great) and shallots. Top with the Superfood Sprinkle, drizzle with olive oil and lemon juice, and season with salt and pepper to taste.

Superfood Sprinkle

Makes 2-1/2 cups

We all know how healthy superfood seeds like hemp and chia are, but sometimes reaching for various bags can be a hassle when we're rushing. This Superfood Sprinkle makes it easy to add an extra nutritional boost to oats, yogurt, smoothies, and almost any other dish you can think of!

½ cup hemp hearts

½ cup chia seeds

½ cup sunflower seeds

½ cup pumpkin seeds

½ raw buckwheat groats

Combine all of the ingredients in a Mason jar. Alternatively, if a fine texture is preferred, grind the ingredients in a food processor for a few minutes. Sprinkle the mixture on oats, yogurt, fruit, or salads. Keeps well for up to 1 month in a cool, dark place or in the fridge.

CREAMY AVOCADO-CUCUMBER ROLLS

Makes 10 to 12 rolls

I love fresh, delicious little party plates! These cucumber rolls are perfectly crunchy and smooth, with a great fresh taste of cucumber and a creamy avocado spread. This is one delicious crowd-pleaser for people who are a little health conscious, people who have allergies (this is very allergen friendly), and people who will eat just about anything. A little something good for you will do you good!

2 large English cucumbers, peeled

3 ripe avocados, pitted and peeled

¼ cup capers, plus more for garnish

¼ cup fresh parsley or dill, finely chopped, plus more for garnish

2 tablespoons freshly squeezed lemon juice

½ teaspoon Himalayan pink or sea salt

Freshly cracked black pepper

Use a mandoline to cut thin cucumber slices all the way down the length of each cucumber. Keep slicing until you reach the wider area near the center of each cucumber. Be careful to not break the slices, if possible.

In a bowl, mush the avocados. Add the capers, parsley, lemon juice, and salt and pepper to taste and mix to combine.

Lay each cucumber slice down flat and spoon a thin layer of the avocado spread all the way across each slice. Roll up gently from one end. Use extra avocado spread to seal them closed.

Dress up with extra parsley and capers and serve!

NOTES

It's a good idea to grab more cucumbers than you need for this recipe, as some pieces could break on the mandoline. You only use the wide center slices. (The thinner cucumber slices can be saved for a salad or snacked on.)

These are wonderful for summer, but avocado doesn't tolerate the heat well, so be mindful of that. Serve them as appetizers so they're eaten up first, or keep them in the fridge until serving time.

Green Collard Wraps

Serves 4

Using fresh green collard leaves as a wrap is amazingly healthy and so fresh to bite into. You will love these for lunch, a light dinner, or even as a party platter! If you are serving them for a crowd, consider prepping all the ingredients on plates and bowls for a DIY wrap bar. It's so much more fun and less work for you. Win!

4 large collard leaves

1 carrot

1 English cucumber

½ daikon radish

½ cup Vegenaise or Raw Veggie Pâté (page 44)

1 avocado, pitted, peeled, and sliced

Handful of pea shoots or any sprouts

Tamarind Dipping Sauce, for serving (recipe follows)

Place the collard greens on a flat surface, and cut away the top portion of the tough stems by sliding the knife parallel to the leaf. Cut the carrot, cucumber, and radish into matchsticks—a julienne peeler makes this easy or just use a knife.

Spread the mayonnaise on the collard leaves and top with the veggies, avocado, and sprouts. Roll each leaf with fillings tightly to make a wrap. Cut into bite sizes or in half. Use toothpicks to keep wraps from unravelling. Enjoy with the Tamarind Dipping Sauce.

Tamarind Dipping Sauce

Serves 4

½ cup Vegenaise

⅓ cup tamarind sauce

Mix the mayonnaise and tamarind sauce in a small bowl. Great for dipping collard wraps or veggie burgers like the Lentil Burgers (page 102) or adding to sandwiches for a great flavor boost.

Soups

Beet & Adzuki Bean Soup

Serves 4

Since childhood, beets have always made a regular appearance on our dinner table, but it wasn't until more recently that I appreciated them for their amazing health properties. This is a delicious beet soup that uses the whole beet, from root to tip (no waste or questioning what to do with those leaves). It pairs well with adzuki or black beans to make for a protein-rich, hearty, and delicious soup.

Grapeseed oil, for cooking

1 medium onion, chopped

2 cloves garlic, chopped

3 quarts water, heated

4 medium beets with their greens, beets peeled and diced, greens chopped

1 medium carrot, chopped

1 parsnip, chopped

¼ celery root, chopped

3 bay leaves

1 teaspoon caraway seeds

1 (15-ounce) can adzuki or black beans

¾ tablespoon sea salt

Freshly ground black pepper

Chopped scallions, for serving

In a large pot, drizzle a bit of oil to coat the bottom and sauté the onions over medium heat until translucent. Add the garlic and continue cooking for a few minutes, stirring often. Add the water, beets, carrots, parsnip, celery root, bay leaves, and caraway seeds. Cook for 15 to 20 minutes, until the vegetables are soft. Stir in the beans and season with the salt and pepper. Cook for another 5 minutes. Remove the bay leaves before serving. Serve topped with the scallions.

HEARTY MISO SOUP

Serves 4

Any time you want a deliciously slurpy comfort-food bowl of soup, this is the soup for you. Miso paste is made from fermented soybean and helps to repopulate the good bacteria in the stomach. A jar of it also keeps for months in the fridge, which makes it easy and convenient to throw these ingredients together in a pot and make this in no time.

½ (10-ounce) package rice or soba noodles

Sesame oil, for frying and coating noodles

¾ cup cubed firm tofu

2 or 3 cloves garlic, minced

1 carrot, cut into matchsticks

3 or 4 stalks baby bok choy, coarsely chopped

6 tablespoons miso paste

1 to 2 teaspoons Asian hot sauce (optional)

½ cup dried seaweed, such as nori or wakame

Chopped scallions, for topping

Sesame seeds, for topping

Bring a large pot filled with salted water to a boil, and cook the rice noodles as directed. Drain in a colander, toss with sesame oil to prevent from sticking, and set aside.

In another pot, heat the sesame oil over medium heat and fry the tofu until golden on both sides. Remove from the pot and set aside in a bowl. Add the garlic to the same pot and sauté for just a minute, until a little golden color appears. Remove from the pot and add to the tofu. Pour in enough hot water to fill the pot (10 to 12 cups; use boiling water from a kettle). Add the carrots, bok choy, and miso paste and stir well to dissolve and incorporate the miso. Season with hot sauce to taste. Cook for about 5 to 10 minutes; you don't want to overcook the vegetables. Add the noodles, stir in the tofu and garlic, and add the seaweed.

Serve immediately in bowls, topped with scallions and sesame seeds.

BRUSSELS SPROUT, PEA & FRESH DILL SOUP

Serves 4

Keep to simple, pure ingredients and enjoy a little soup heaven. These spring vegetables come together so beautifully, and the dill is the key to freshness here! I usually like to add a protein source to most of my meals so they are heartier. Lentils are packed with protein, fiber, and lots of nutrition, and they are the secret ingredient that adds creaminess to this delicious soup. Be ready to go back for seconds.

1 cup dried split red lentils

Grapeseed oil, for cooking

1 medium onion, chopped

3 medium carrots, chopped

2 medium potatoes, peeled and diced

1 medium parsnip, chopped

¼ celery root, chopped

1 cup shredded cabbage

3 quarts water, heated

10 brussels sprouts

1 cup frozen peas

Sea salt and freshly cracked black pepper

Handful of fresh dill, chopped

Bring a medium pot of water to a boil and cook the lentils as instructed.

Meanwhile, in a large pot over medium heat, drizzle in some oil to cover the bottom, add the onions, and sauté until slightly golden. Add the carrots, potatoes, parsnips, celery root, and cabbage and cook for about 5 minutes, stirring occasionally so they don't stick to the bottom of the pot. Add more oil if need be if the oil gets absorbed too much. Once the veggies are slightly golden, slowly pour in the hot water, about 1 cup at a time, while mixing the vegetables. Bring to a boil, then cover, decrease the heat, and cook for another 5 minutes, stirring occasionally. Add the brussels sprouts and peas and cook for another 5 minutes.

Purée the cooked lentils to a smooth paste and stir into the soup. (This is that magic step that makes this soup nice and creamy). Season with salt and pepper to taste and serve sprinkled with fresh dill on top.

Moroccan Vegetable & Chickpea Stew

Serves 6 to 8

This is a very easy one-pot meal that I've loved for years, especially in the colder months, as all these ingredients, especially the spices, are naturally warming to the body. This stew tastes even better the next day, when all the flavors get fully absorbed and it becomes even creamier. So make sure you make enough for at least two meals. If you have a big family, double up the ingredients to make a huge pot of this great healthy veggie stew.

Grapeseed oil, for cooking

2 medium onions, diced

3 or 4 sweet potatoes, peeled and chopped

1 green bell pepper, chopped

1½ teaspoons curry powder

1 teaspoon sea salt

½ teaspoon ground cumin

½ teaspoon ground turmeric

¼ teaspoon freshly ground black pepper

¼ teaspoon red pepper flakes

1 (28-ounce) can chopped tomatoes

1 (19-ounce) can chickpeas, rinsed and drained

¼ cup chopped fresh cilantro

Prepare a kettle of water to bring to a boil. In a large pot over medium-low heat, drizzle in some oil to cover the bottom and sauté the onions until translucent. Add the sweet potatoes and bell peppers, stir, and sauté for about 10 minutes. Add more oil if needed so the veggies don't stick to the pan.

Add in all of the spices and continue to cook for about 10 minutes. Decrease the heat and slowly pour in some of the hot water to cover the vegetables while stirring the pot. Allow those vegetables to absorb some of the water by cooking for about 5 more minutes, and then add about 2 more cups of the hot water to the pot. Stir again and add the tomatoes and chickpeas. (The consistency should be that of a stew and not a watery soup.) Ten to 12 cups of water altogether should work well, but a bit less water makes the stew chunkier, so adjust the consistency to your liking.

To serve, top with the cilantro. It also freezes well in an airtight container for up to 3 months.

Butter Bean, Kale & Tomato Soup

Serves 4 to 6

This is my go-to recipe that brings instant satisfaction and comfort every time. It's a hearty soup of all my favorite ingredients that, when combined, create the best bean soup ever. It's also a recipe that I can quickly make when our fridge is nearly empty because it uses basic staple vegetables, fresh or frozen kale, dried beans, and a can of tomato paste, which I always keep in my pantry. Sometimes the hardest part is to remember to soak the beans in the morning. After that, it's all throw-in-the-pot and before you know it, a hearty, delicious dinner is ready.

1 cup (19-ounce can) dried large white beans

3 quarts water

Grapeseed or other neutral oil, for cooking

1 medium onion, chopped

2 medium carrots, chopped

1 parsnip, chopped

1 celery stalk, chopped

1 tablespoon dried marjoram

1 cup chopped kale or spinach (frozen works great)

1 (12-ounce) can tomato paste

2¼ teaspoons sea salt

Freshly ground black pepper

Fresh flat-leaf parsley leaves, for serving

Soak the beans in water to cover for 6 to 12 hours.

Rinse and drain the beans and place in a large pot filled with 3 quarts water. Bring to a boil, then lower the heat to simmer, add salt, and cook the beans for 30 to 45 minutes, until soft. (For quicker turnaround time, use canned beans.)

Heat some oil in a skillet over medium heat and sauté the onions until golden.

When the beans start to soften, add the sautéed onions, carrots, parsnips, celery, and marjoram and stir, then cook for 5 to 10 minutes. Add the kale and tomato paste, and continue cooking for 5 to 10 minutes. Season with black pepper to taste.

Serve hot, sprinkled with parsley.

TEX-MEX SPICY CHILI

Serves 4 to 6

I love comfort-food dishes that are hearty, filling, and just hit the spot (especially on those cold days). This recipe has a meaty texture and the heartiness of a chili I used to love, and it's been my mission to re-create that perfect bowl of goodness for a long time. This does not disappoint; my husband approves of it, too.

Grapeseed or mustard oil, for cooking

1 teaspoon fennel seeds

2 medium onions, coarsely chopped

1 celery stalk, chopped

1 (19-ounce) can red kidney beans

1 (28-ounce) can diced tomatoes

½ cup frozen corn

2 cups TVP (textured vegetable protein), or 1 cup dried red split lentils

4 to 6 cups boiling water

1 teaspoon cumin seeds

1 teaspoon cayenne pepper

1 tablespoon dried oregano

1 tablespoon dried basil

1 tablespoon garlic powder

½ teaspoon freshly ground black pepper

Sea salt

Scallions, chopped, for serving

Avocado, chopped, for serving

Lime wedges, for serving

Place a large pot over medium heat and drizzle in some oil. Add the fennel seeds, onions, and celery and cook for about 5 minutes. Add the beans, tomatoes, and corn and stir. Add the TVP, along with 4 cups of the boiling water and stir to combine. Add all of the spices and stir, then cover and cook for about 10 minutes. Taste and season with more salt, black pepper, and cayenne, if you like.

Serve hot, topped with scallions and avocado, with lime wedges on the side.

Mains & Sides

Zucchini Noodles with Spinach Pesto & Cherry Tomatoes

Serves 1

Zucchini noodles are the best thing, an even better "invention" than sliced bread! I still get giddy with excitement as I watch the "zoodles" come out the other side of my spiral slicer. They are a real game-changer. I used to be a big pasta lover (anything with carbs!). Now it's amazing that I can enjoy my favorite dishes but reinvented in a healthier way with great delicious flavors. This is my go-to recipe for a quick "zoodle" dish. The homemade spinach pesto is so easy and quick to make and is simply divine.

4 large zucchini

Spinach Pesto (recipe follows)

1 pint cherry tomatoes, halved

With a spiral slicer or julienne peeler, make noodles from the zucchini. Place in a large bowl, toss with the pesto and tomatoes, and serve.

Spinach Pesto

Serves 1

4 handfuls fresh spinach, stemmed

Handful of fresh basil, stemmed

2 tablespoons raw pine nuts

2 tablespoons slivered or chopped raw almonds

1 clove garlic, peeled

¼ cup olive oil

2 tablespoons freshly squeezed lemon juice

Sea salt and freshly cracked black pepper

Place all of the ingredients in a food processor and process until a paste forms.

BAKED ZUCCHINI BOATS

Serves 4 to 6

This is a big hit from the *Pure Ella* blog! A dish that does not disappoint, it has made many people's dinners so much healthier and happier.

3 large zucchini, halved lengthwise

2 large tomatoes, finely diced

Kale-Spinach Pesto (recipe follows)

Sea salt and freshly ground black pepper

½ cup gluten-free bread crumbs

Fresh basil leaves, for serving

Grapeseed oil

Preheat the oven to 350°F.

With a spoon or ice cream scoop (because that's more fun!), scoop out the soft inner flesh of the zucchini. Oil the hollowed-out shells all over and set aside in a baking dish.

Chop the zucchini flesh into small pieces and put in a large bowl. Add the tomatoes and kale-spinach pesto, and mix with a wooden spoon to combine. Season with salt and pepper to taste. Fill the zucchini shells with the mixture, sprinkle with the bread crumbs, and bake for 30 to 40 minutes or until tops appear golden. Serve sprinkled with basil leaves.

 NOTE These zucchini boats are also great for large crowds if you can cut them into quarters.

Veggie Protein Tacos

Serves 2 or 3

These tacos are so amazing and quick to put together, you and your whole family will love them! Best of all, the cooking is so minimal and easy. Corn tacos are naturally gluten-free (but I do recommend getting organic, as corn is one of the top GMO foods).

Filling and Shells

1 cup TVP (textured vegetable protein)

¼ to ½ cup water

1 to 2 teaspoons chili powder*

½ teaspoon garlic powder*

¼ teaspoon onion powder*

½ teaspoon paprika*

1½ teaspoons ground cumin powder*

2 teaspoons fine sea salt

1 teaspoon freshly ground black pepper

8 to 10 corn hard taco shells (organic, if possible)

Toppings

Romaine lettuce, finely chopped

Tomato, finely chopped

Red onion, finely chopped

Avocado-Lime Cream (page 74)

* or substitute all these for 2 tablespoons all-natural taco seasoning

In a medium skillet or pot, mix the vegetable protein with the water and all of the seasonings and heat over medium-high for about 5 minutes. Add a few tablespoons more water if the "meat" looks too dry. Transfer to a serving bowl.

For the best, most fun way to eat, set the taco shells, taco filling, Avocado-Lime Cream, and all the toppings in the middle of the table for a self-serve taco station.

Everybody helps themselves and enjoys a delicious, protein-rich, light-tasting, healthy, taco night!

Avocado-Lime Cream

Serves 2 or 3

2 avocados

Juice of 1 lime

3 tablespoons avocado oil or extra-virgin olive oil

2 tablespoons finely chopped red onion

Sea salt and freshly ground black pepper

Halve the avocados and scoop out the flesh into a bowl. Add all of the remaining ingredients and mix with a fork, smashing the avocado until it is a creamy consistency.

Zucchini Pasta with Wild Rice Veggie Balls

Serves 4

If you love delicious comfort-food meals, like classic spaghetti and meatballs, then you're going to love this healthier version with zucchini noodles and veggie balls. To save time, cook the wild rice the night before, as it takes about 45 minutes.

Spaghetti Sauce

Your favorite store-bought marinara sauce

Or to make your own

4 tomatoes, chopped

2 tablespoons grapeseed oil

2 teaspoons Italian seasonings, such as dried basil and oregano

Sea salt and freshly ground black pepper

Wild Rice Veggie Balls

Grapeseed oil or neutral oil of your choice, for cooking

1 small onion, finely chopped

1 carrot, finely chopped

¾ cup chopped white mushrooms

3 cloves garlic, minced

1 cup cooked and cooled wild or brown rice

½ cup raw walnuts

⅓ cup fresh flat-leaf parsley

1 teaspoon dried thyme

1 to 2 teaspoons fine sea salt

½ to 1 teaspoon freshly cracked black pepper

½ teaspoon cayenne pepper

About ⅓ cup chickpea flour or other flour, for coating

To serve

½ (16-ounce) package gluten-free brown rice pasta

3 medium zucchini

Extra-virgin olive oil, for drizzling

1 cup marinara sauce, for serving

Fresh herbs, such as basil or thyme, for topping

Continued

If making your own tomato sauce, simply cook the tomatoes with the oil and seasonings in a small pot over medium heat, stirring occasionally so it doesn't burn. If it sticks, add a little bit of water. Total cooking time should be 5 to 10 minutes. Turn off the heat and cover to keep warm.

For the wild rice veggie balls: Heat a large saucepan over medium heat with a bit of oil, and sauté the onions and carrots until they start to soften. Add the mushrooms and garlic and cook for about 5 minutes. Set aside to cool.

In a food processor, combine the rice, walnuts, parsley, thyme, salt, black pepper, and cayenne. Process to a crumbly mixture. Turn off the processor halfway through and scrape down the sides. Taste a little and adjust the seasoning to your liking. When the mixture is ready, remove the blade and get ready to make some balls!

On a large plate, spread out the chickpea flour. Scoop some of the dough, about the size of a golf ball, onto the palm of your hand and roll to make a ball. Then roll in the flour and dust off some of the extra flour that may stick on.

Heat a large cast-iron pan over medium heat with some oil. Cook the no-meat balls, rolling them around every minute or so to brown them evenly. Don't roll too soon, as the balls might stick to the pan if they're not cooked on that side yet. You're looking for a little golden color before you roll them to another side.

Meanwhile, as the balls are cooking, cook the pasta according to the package directions. Use a spiralizer (spiral slicer) or julienne peeler to cut the zucchini into noodles. Drain the pasta and drizzle with olive oil, stirring to coat well. Cover to keep warm.

Just before serving, toss the zucchini noodles with the pasta. Top with the veggie balls and tomato sauce. Finish with a sprinkle of fresh herbs.

HERBED TOFU-STUFFED MINI PEPPERS

Serves 4 to 6

These beautiful tricolored mini peppers are so delicious. The peppers take on this incredible creamy taste when stuffed with herbed organic tofu and baked—so simple to do, yet so great to devour. They are also amazing on the grill too.

10 to 12 mini tricolored peppers (red, orange, and yellow)

Grapeseed oil or neutral oil of your choice, for cooking

1 medium onion, diced

½ zucchini, finely chopped

1 or 2 cloves garlic, minced

1½ cups cubed firm tofu

¼ cup almond milk, or 3 tablespoons Vegenaise

1 teaspoon dried basil

1 teaspoon dried oregano

1 teaspoon fresh thyme

½ to 1 tablespoon sea salt

½ teaspoon sweet paprika

Freshly cracked black pepper

Pinch of cayenne pepper

Fresh basil leaves, for serving

Preheat the oven to 350°F and line a baking sheet with parchment paper.

Cut the ends off the peppers and scoop out the insides with a small spoon. Reserve the tops with stems and set aside.

In a frying pan over medium-low heat, sauté the onions in a bit of oil until golden. (Any black spots will add a bitter taste to the dish, so keep stirring often and keep the heat fairly low.) Add the zucchini and garlic and cook together until all is softened, adding more oil if needed. Set aside to cool slightly.

In a food processor, pulse the tofu until it crumbles. Add the zucchini mixture, milk, basil, oregano, thyme, salt, paprika, black pepper, and cayenne. Pulse more to combine all the ingredients, but don't overmix, as some texture from the onions and zucchini is great. Taste the mixture and adjust the seasoning to your liking.

Fill the peppers with the tofu mixture, place on the baking sheet, and drizzle with oil, rubbing the oil on all sides of the peppers. Sprinkle with extra seasoning as desired. Bake for 30 to 40 minutes, carefully turning the peppers over once halfway through the cooking time. Serve hot or warm, sprinkled with basil leaves.

Spaghetti Squash Bounty Salad

Serves 4 to 6

Spaghetti squash is such an ingenious vegetable. Isn't it clever to grow spaghetti strands inside a squash? This dish is great and healthy and tastes amazing. It makes a great side dish, or sometimes I add lentils and it literally becomes a meal in minutes. Once you prebake the squash, it becomes a very quick and easy dish to put together. It's also very versatile year-round and goes with everything.

1 large spaghetti squash

¼ cup olive oil, plus more for rubbing the squash

½ cup raw pine nuts

1 pint cherry tomatoes, halved

1 large cucumber, cubed

¼ medium red onion, finely chopped

Juice of ½ lemon

1 tablespoon celery seeds

2 teaspoons sea salt

Freshly cracked black pepper

Preheat the oven to 350°F.

Cut the spaghetti squash in half lengthwise, scoop out the seeds, and rub the inside of the squash with olive oil. Place on a baking sheet and bake for 30 to 45 minutes.

Let cool slightly. Using a fork, scrape the spaghetti strings out completely into a large bowl, leaving only the skin. Lower the oven temperature to 200°F and line a small baking sheet with parchment paper.

Place the pine nuts on the parchment-lined baking sheet and toast them lightly in the oven at 200°F for 5 minutes, or until golden brown. Toss them halfway through baking. Be careful not to burn them, as they brown really quickly.

Add the tomatoes, cucumbers, onions, lemon juice, the ¼ cup olive oil, celery seeds, salt, and pepper to the spaghetti squash strings and toss to combine. Top with the pine nuts just before serving.

Black Bean–Tomato Tart

Serves 3 or 4

This pastry dough recipe makes enough for two tarts. Make one tart with these ingredients and have fun changing up the ingredients on the other tart. Or freeze the second half until next time.

1 (17-ounce) package gluten-free or spelt puff pastry or make your own (recipe follows)

Pastry (ingredients for 2 tarts)

2⅓ cups all-purpose gluten-free flour or light spelt flour

½ cup vegan shortening, cold

½ cup vegan buttery spread, cold

Up to ½ cup ice water

1 teaspoon freshly ground black pepper

2 teaspoons fine sea salt

1 teaspoon garlic powder

1 teaspoon onion powder

2 tablespoons chopped fresh rosemary

Toppings

2 large tomatoes, sliced

¼ red onion, thinly sliced

½ cup cooked black beans, rinsed and drained

2 tablespoons extra-virgin olive oil

Sea salt and freshly ground black pepper

Fresh rosemary leaves

To make the pastry: Sift the flour into a large bowl, add the shortening and butter and cut it with a pastry cutter or in a food processor. Once crumbles form, transfer the dough to a work surface, create a well, and slowly pour in the ice water, just a little at a time. Continue folding and cutting and adding water a few tablespoons at a time until a dough forms. Knead in the seasoning and fresh rosemary. Do not overwork. Little dots of unincorporated shortening/butter are necessary for lightness. Kneading for 3 to 4 minutes should be perfect. If the dough feels warm or soft, cool in the fridge or freezer for just a few minutes. Divide the dough into two balls. Wrap each in plastic wrap and keep cool in the refrigerator before assembling the tart.

Preheat the oven to 400°F.

Lay a sheet of parchment paper on a baking sheet. Press one dough ball with your fingers or a rolling pin into a rectangle about ½ inch thick.

Drizzle the tart with a little olive oil and scatter the tomato, onion, black beans, and fresh rosemary. Brush the top with the remaining olive oil. Bake for 25 to 35 minutes, until golden.

Cabbage Roll Casserole

Serves 4 to 6

Because of my Eastern European roots, I'm no stranger to cabbage rolls. And it's great to finally see cabbage renowned as a superfood and be put on the map. This recipe takes the traditional tastes of cabbage rolls and simplifies them into an easy, no-fuss, layered dish that everyone will love.

1 head green cabbage

Sea salt

½ cup buckwheat groats

½ cup white (not instant) or brown rice

Grapeseed oil for cooking

2 medium onions, diced

1 large carrot, diced

1 cup TVP (textured vegetable protein)

1 (6-ounce) can tomato paste

Freshly ground black pepper

1 (28-ounce) can diced tomatoes

1 tablespoon dried marjoram (or dried thyme or oregano)

Remove any wilted outer leaves from the cabbage. With a sharp knife, trim away some of the inner core (this will remove the toughest parts of the stems and make it easier to pull the leaves apart). Place the whole head in a large pot, fill the pot with water, and bring to a simmer over medium-high heat. Simmer for 10 minutes, then gently pour out the water and let the cabbage cool.

Fill a medium pot with water and 1 teaspoon salt and bring to a boil. Check the cooking instructions on the buckwheat groats and rice packaging; they should cook in the same amount of time. Add the buckwheat and rice to the boiling water and cook per the instructions (together is fine). When cooked, drain and set aside.

Meanwhile, as the cabbage and rice-buckwheat are cooking, start the cabbage roll filling.

Continued

In a large sauté pan, heat a bit of oil over medium-low heat and sauté the onions until lightly golden brown. Add the carrots and continue cooking for about 3 minutes. Add the TVP, at which time you will need to add about 1 cup of water—enough that the TVP isn't sticking to the bottom of the pan, but you don't want it runny. Mix in the tomato paste and season with salt and pepper to taste.

By now the rice and buckwheat should be cooked. Drain and add to the TVP mixture. Mix well to combine and season again to your liking.

Preheat the oven to 350°F.

To assemble, pour a little water into a 12-inch or larger casserole dish, to just barely cover the bottom. (This will prevent the cabbage from sticking and burning.) Pull the leaves off the cabbage. If some leaves tear, not to worry. Lay the first layer of cabbage in the casserole. In all you will have three cabbage layers. Use the smaller inner leaves in the middle and reserve the larger outer pieces for the bottom and top. This will create a nicer-looking top and it will be easier to cut and serve, as the fuller top and bottom layers will help hold the slices together.

Spread half the TVP-rice-buckwheat mixture on the bottom cabbage layer. Top with a layer of cabbage and then with the remaining TVP mixture. Top with the final cabbage layer, then the diced tomatoes, marjoram, and salt and pepper to taste.

Bake, uncovered, for 15 to 20 minutes. This dish is already fully cooked, but baking helps the flavors mingle together. Allow to rest for about 10 minutes before serving. This dish is even better the next day, as the flavors soak together and it is easier to cut clean wedges that don't fall apart.

NOTE You can also freeze this dish for up to 3 months. Thaw in the refrigerator overnight or for about 5 hours, then bake and serve. Or portion into small servings and freeze those, for an even faster thawing time.

Classic Falafel with Tahini Sauce

Serves 4

If you think making your own falafel from scratch is complicated, it is so not so. This is honestly one of the simplest recipes I've ever done, and it turns out perfectly every time. My husband and daughter beg for falafel all the time and I happily oblige. Homemade falafel is versatile in salads and wraps but is also great for added protein in lunches for school or work. It's a big crowd-pleaser for potlucks and family dinners, too.

1½ cups dried chickpeas, soaked in water for at least 6 hours

3 cloves garlic, peeled

1 small onion, coarsely chopped

¼ cup chopped fresh flat-leaf parsley

1 tablespoon tapioca starch or any starch or your choice, such as potato starch or cornstarch

2 teaspoons ground cumin

1½ teaspoons sea salt

1 teaspoon ground coriander

Freshly cracked black pepper

½ cup grapeseed oil or neutral oil of your choice

Tahini Sauce, for serving (recipe follows)

Drain the chickpeas and place in a food processor. Add the garlic, onion, parsley, tapioca, cumin, salt, coriander, and pepper to taste. Process on high speed until everything is well blended. Halfway through, turn off the processor and scrape down the sides to incorporate all the ingredients.

Remove the blade from the processor bowl. Scoop a spoonful of mixture into your hand and shape into a ball or egg. Continue with all the mixture.

Heat a frying pan over medium heat and add oil. To test the oil, simply drop in a tiny piece of the chickpea mixture; if the oil gently bubbles around it, you're good to go. If it just sits there, give it more time to heat up. If it makes cracking noises and bubbles strongly, it is too hot. Adjust your heat accordingly.

Continued

Drop the falafel balls in gently; do not throw them, as that could cause splattering and you might get burned. Put in as many as can fit without crowding. You should be able to move them around and flip them and they should not overlap. Cook for about 3 minutes on the first side. Look for a golden yellow color. Gently flip with a long fork or tongs and cook on the other side, about 2 minutes. Remove with a slotted spatula or spoon and drain on a paper towel–lined plate. Serve with the tahini sauce.

Tahini Sauce

½ cup tahini

3 cloves garlic, crushed

½ teaspoon fine sea salt

2 tablespoons extra-virgin olive oil

Juice of ½ lemon

1 teaspoon finely chopped fresh flat-leaf parsley (optional)

In a food processor or a small bowl, combine all of the ingredients. If mixing in a bowl, be sure your garlic is minced very finely. If the sauce is too thick, add a teaspoon warm water and blend until the sauce is a little thinner. The sauce will keep in an airtight container in the refrigerator for up to 5 days.

Meaty but Meatless Spaghetti

Serves 4 to 6

This is my go-to for the quickest meal at our house. Spaghetti is everyone's favorite (of course), so it's great to make it with an alternative vegetable protein that is so convenient and less expensive to use than meat. I have a bag of organic TVP in the cupboard at all times and use it to whip up this dinner on busy days. This sauce is so rich and authentic that even my husband loves this dish as well as the kids.

Sea salt

½ (16-ounce) package gluten-free brown rice pasta

Grapeseed oil or neutral oil of your choice, for cooking

1 large onion, diced

2 kale leaves, stemmed and chopped

2 tomatoes, diced

1 head broccoli, cut into small florets

1 cup TVP (textured vegetable protein) or 1 (19-ounce) can lentils, rinsed and drained

1½ cups marinara sauce

About 1 cup boiling water, as needed

Extra-virgin olive oil, for drizzling

Raw pine nuts, for serving (optional)

Fresh basil leaves, for serving (optional)

Bring a large pot of water to a boil, add ½ tablespoon salt, and cook the pasta according to the package directions.

In a large pan, heat a bit of grapeseed oil over medium heat and sauté the onions until slightly golden, about 2 minutes. Add the kale, tomatoes, and broccoli, cover, and cook for another 2 minutes. If the vegetables stick to the pan, add a little hot water at a time, stir, and cover to continue to steam-cook.

Once the vegetables are softened but not fully cooked, add the TVP and marinara sauce. Stir well to combine all the ingredients. If the sauce looks too dry (because the TVP absorbs a lot of liquid), add about ¼ cup of the boiling water at a time to make it the right saucy consistency. Turn off the heat and cover for another couple of minutes to let it finish cooking.

About this time, the pasta should be ready. Drain, rinse with a little water to remove some starch, and toss with a little olive oil.

Distribute the pasta among large bowls and top with the spaghetti sauce, plus a little sprinkle of pine nuts and basil leaves. Enjoy immediately!

WILD RICE BURGERS

Serves 4 to 6

These meatless burgers are hearty and delicious! Wild rice is my favorite; it's so versatile and delicious on its own or incorporated into a recipe. These eggplant "buns" are my favorite way to replace real buns. Grab a fork and knife for this one and enjoy.

Grapeseed or other neutral oil, for cooking

1 medium onion, finely diced

⅓ cup uncooked wild rice (1 cup cooked)

1 cup cooked black beans

1 chia or flax "egg" (mix 1 tablespoon ground chia or ground flax seeds with 2 tablespoons warm water and let stand for 2 minutes)

1 to 2 teaspoons sea salt

1 to 2 teaspoons freshly cracked black pepper

½ to 1 teaspoon ground turmeric

½ teaspoon chili powder (optional)

½ teaspoon dried oregano

Up to ½ cup rice flour or other flour, to coat burger patties

NOTE Wild rice cooks in about 1 hour, so it's a timesaver to cook the rice the night before or otherwise plan ahead. (I often freeze cooked rice for a quick thaw to use the day of.) If you're cooking the beans yourself, be sure to allow for that time also. Cooking your own beans is healthier, more economical, and ecofriendly. But convenience helps a ton; if you are using canned beans, just look for BPA-free cans if possible.

In a large nonstick skillet, heat a bit of oil over medium-low heat and sauté the onion until golden. Set aside.

In a food processor, blend the wild rice, black beans, chia "egg," and spices. I like to leave some texture so I blend for just a few seconds to get a crumbly but sticky mixture. Transfer to a bowl, add the onions, and mix to incorporate. Taste and adjust the seasonings to your liking.

Dust a plate with the flour. Form a heaping tablespoon of the mixture into a patty, and coat the patty in the flour. Prepare all the burgers, then heat some oil in the same pan you used to sauté the onions. Cook the burgers for 2 to 3 minutes on one side on medium heat, or until slightly golden and firmed, then flip and cook the other side. You don't want to handle them too much or they could crumble or stick to the pan. Add more oil if needed and continue with the rest of the patties.

Serve the burgers in a bun or on a salad. Or my favorite way: stacked on grilled slices of eggplant with kale, pickled red pepper, vegan mayo, grainy mustard, and ketchup.

Tex-Mex Quinoa–Sweet Potato Boats

Serves 4

This is a great dish that is a balance of both comfort food and freshness. Baked sweet potatoes topped with the delicious Tex-Mex salsa flavors of black beans, corn, and cilantro will excite your taste buds, y'all!

4 sweet potatoes

Grapeseed or other neutral oil, for the potatoes

Tex-Mex Quinoa Salsa

½ cup cooked quinoa (great to use leftovers)

1 cup corn kernels, frozen or canned

½ medium red onion, chopped

1 small red bell pepper, chopped

1 (15-ounce) can black beans, rinsed and drained

2 teaspoons ground cumin

½ teaspoon cayenne pepper

½ cup chopped fresh cilantro

Sea salt and freshly ground black pepper

Preheat the oven to 350°F and line a baking sheet with parchment paper. Pat the sweet potatoes dry and oil them. Place on the baking sheet and bake for 30 to 45 minutes. Set aside to cool.

To make the salsa, bring a medium pot of water to a boil, and cook the quinoa per the package instructions. Near the end, add the corn to finish cooking at the same time.

Drain and transfer to a bowl.

Mix in the red onion, bell pepper, black beans, cumin, cayenne, and some of the cilantro (reserve some cilantro for garnish). Season with salt and pepper to taste.

Slice the tops off the sweet potatoes, open them up a bit, and scoop out some of the soft flesh. Fill the sweet potato shells with the Tex-Mex Quinoa Salsa and top with the reserved cilantro.

NOTE You will have extra Tex-Mex Quinoa Salsa left over to serve as a stand-alone side dish or for lunch the next day.

QUINOA TABBOULEH

Serves 4 to 6

Healthy foods rule, and if kale is king, then quinoa must be queen! In this dish, these superfoods come together perfectly. This is my favorite kind of "salad" because it goes so well with everything and packs great for lunches, picnics, and barbecues. Grilled zucchini and sweet potato on the side are always a good idea.

½ teaspoon sea salt, plus more for seasoning

1 cup quinoa

1 English cucumber, chopped

1 small red bell pepper, chopped

1 pint cherry tomatoes, halved

¼ cup chopped red onion

½ cup chopped fresh flat-leaf parsley

½ cup chopped fresh mint

Juice of ½ lemon

¼ cup extra-virgin olive oil

Freshly ground black pepper

In a medium saucepan, bring about 1½ cups water to a boil with ½ teaspoon salt and add the quinoa. Decrease the heat to medium-low, cover, and simmer until the quinoa is tender, 10 to 15 minutes. Remove from the heat and let stand for 5 minutes, covered. Stir and fluff with a fork and set aside to cool.

In a large bowl, combine the cucumber, bell pepper, tomatoes, red onion, parsley, and mint. Mix in the quinoa. Drizzle in the lemon juice and olive oil and season to taste with salt and pepper.

NOTE Serve as is as a salad or side dish. It is delicious with roasted sweet potato and zucchini slices. Add beans or lentils for a fuller meal.

Chickpea Flatbread Pizza
with Roasted Garlic, Arugula & Capers

Makes two 8-inch pizzas

Pizza lovers, hold up! This crust is perfection beyond belief: crispy, light, and not only gluten-free but grain-free, too! Also, this is loaded with hidden protein—quite amazing for a veggie pizza! And the crust doubles as a great flatbread sidekick for soup or hummus. Your mouth will say "Wow!"

1 cup chickpea flour

¾ cup water

½ cup extra-virgin olive oil, divided, plus more for drizzling

4 heads garlic

1 cup canned chickpeas (rinsed and drained)

1 teaspoon dried oregano

1 teaspoon dried basil

1 teaspoon fine sea salt

¼ teaspoon black pepper

Toppings

Sun-dried tomatoes

Capers

Arugula

½ cup cooked chickpeas

In a medium bowl, mix the flour, water, and ¼ cup of the oil. Set aside at room temperature for 1 hour or refrigerate overnight.

Preheat the oven to 400°F. Slice off the garlic head tips, peel the skins (leaving the heads intact), drizzle them with the remaining ¼ cup oil and wrap them in parchment paper. Place the garlic on a baking sheet and roast for 45 minutes, until the centers are soft. Push the cloves out into a bowl, mash with a fork, and season with salt and pepper to taste.

Increase the oven to 450°F. Line a baking sheet with parchment paper and drizzle oil on top.

Combine the chickpeas, flour mixture, oregano, basil, salt, and pepper on high speed in a food processor until a smooth batter forms. Pour half the batter on one side of the baking sheet, and the remaining half on the other side, to make two 8-inch disks.

Bake for 15 to 20 minutes, until the sides turn golden and the tops look dry.

Spread a layer of roasted garlic, then top with sun-dried tomatoes, capers, arugula, and chickpeas.

Sweet & Spicy Chickpea Curry

Serves 4 to 6

This is one of my favorite comfort foods of all time. It's an easy and quick one-pot dish that will play with your taste buds and make you want to belly dance in your kitchen! I dare you!

Grapeseed or mustard oil, for cooking

1 teaspoon mustard seeds

2 medium onions, chopped

1 teaspoon finely chopped garlic

1 (28-ounce) can diced tomatoes

1 (14-ounce) can chickpeas, rinsed and drained

1 sweet potato, peeled and chopped

2 teaspoons curry powder

1 teaspoon ground turmeric

1 teaspoon ground cumin

½ teaspoon cayenne pepper

½ cup chopped fresh cilantro

Heat a medium pot over medium heat, drizzle in some oil, add the mustard seeds, and cook for 2 to 3 minutes. Add the onions and cook until golden. Add the garlic, tomatoes, chickpeas, sweet potato, curry powder, turmeric, cumin, and cayenne peopper. Continue cooking until the potatoes are soft, about 15 minutes.

Remove the pot from the heat. Using a fork, remove the sweet potatoes and purée or smash with a fork separately. Add the sweet potatoes back to the pot and mix to combine.

Serve hot with cilantro on top. Makes amazing leftovers.

Lentil Burgers with Spicy Tamarind Ketchup

Makes 12 small burgers

Making veggie burgers opens up a world of possibilities. And lentils are so underappreciated. Packed with protein, they stabilize blood sugar, improve digestive health, are good for the heart, and even benefit in weight loss. Beyond all that good-for-you stuff, these lentil burgers are simply amazing when dipped in the tamarind ketchup.

2 cups cooked lentils

1 cup fresh flat-leaf parsley leaves

¼ cup rolled oats

¼ cup chickpea flour

¼ cup raw walnuts (optional)

1 clove garlic, chopped

1 teaspoon ground cumin

¾ teaspoon sea salt

¼ to ½ teaspoon cayenne pepper

Freshly cracked black pepper

2 tablespoons grapeseed oil

Spicy Tamarind Ketchup, for serving (recipe follows)

Preheat the oven to 350°F and line a baking sheet with parchment paper.

Combine all of the ingredients in a food processor and process to incorporate. Shape into golf-sized balls, then press down to make patties and place on the baking sheet. Bake for about 10 minutes on each side. Serve with the spicy ketchup.

Spicy Tamarind Ketchup

Makes 3/4 cup

½ cup ketchup (page 181)

¼ cup tamarind paste

¼ teaspoon cayenne pepper (optional)

Combine all of the ingredients in a bowl and serve. Store in an airtight container in the refrigerator for up to 1 week.

Black Bean, Beet & Spinach Burgers

Makes 8 to 10 burgers

I love turning up the "beet" and boosting nutrition in recipes—that's my thing. These beet burgers are superb in every way, and they are heart healthy and full of protein and fiber. Beets and black beans with a hint of caraway seeds make for a delicious flavor combo.

2 beets, peeled and cooked (1 cup)

1 (15-ounce) can black beans, rinsed and drained

1 cup packed spinach

3 tablespoons potato starch

1 teaspoon dried thyme

½ teaspoon caraway seeds

Sea salt and freshly cracked black pepper

Grapeseed oil, for cooking

Combine the beets, black beans, spinach, potato starch, thyme, caraway seeds, and salt and pepper to taste in a food processor and mix until fully incorporated but with some texture remaining.

Shape into golf ball–size balls and press into patties. Heat a large cast-iron pan to medium, drizzle in some oil, and cook the patties for 3 to 4 minutes on each side.

Serve on top of a salad or as a main course.

Desserts

Mixed Berry Crumble Pots

Serves 4

Berry Crumble is the quickest and easiest dessert you can make. It's one of those recipes you will learn by heart and whip up anytime for a special moment or to wow your friends with your mad baking skills. FYI, you don't need a special occasion to create a special moment. Celebrate life and all the good and delicious things in it.

I like to keep a bag of frozen berries at all times just for moments like this when you need a very quick and freshly homemade dessert.

½ cup rolled oats

½ cup date sugar

½ cup coconut oil, cold

3 cups mixed berries (fresh or frozen)

Preheat oven to 350°F and grease an 8-inch oven-safe deep dish or 4 ramekins.

In a food processor, mix the rolled oats, date sugar, and cold coconut oil for just a few seconds until crumbs form. (You can also mix by hand or use a pastry cutter in a bowl.) To assemble, scatter the berries evenly at the bottom of the dish or in the ramekins and top with the crumble evenly.

Bake for 20 to 30 minutes, until the crumble turns golden. Remove from the oven and allow to cool for 5 minutes before serving.

Serve still hot or cold from the refrigerator. You can also make this crumble in a 6-by-6-inch baking dish, which is better to serve for more people in smaller portions, along with fresh berries.

Raw Brownies with Chocolate Ganache & Pomegranate

Makes 9 squares

Dive into an amazing chocolate treat that's rich and fudgy without the hassle of baking. These are quick and easy to make, literally foolproof. The topping of dark chocolate ganache and sprinkle of pomegranate arils will put your taste buds over the edge! Best of all, the ingredients are so healthy with antioxidants, healthy fats, and protein. Isn't it amazing when a delicious dessert can also be good for you?

1 cup raw walnuts

1 cup raw pecans

1 cup packed Medjool dates, pitted

½ cup almond meal

⅓ cup cocoa powder or raw cacao powder

4 tablespoons coconut oil, melted

¼ cup coconut nectar or maple syrup

2 teaspoons vanilla extract

1 tablespoon ground chia seeds (optional)

Pinch of Himalayan pink or fine sea salt

Chocolate Ganache (recipe follows)

Pomegranate arils, for garnishing

Line an 8-inch square baking dish with parchment paper, keeping the sheet large enough to come up over the sides.

In a food processor, process the walnuts and pecans until fine, about 3 minutes. Add the dates, almond meal, cocoa powder, coconut oil, coconut nectar, vanilla, chia seeds, and salt and continue blending until smooth. Scoop into the prepared baking dish and press with a wooden spoon or your hands to smooth the top.

Place in the refrigerator to set for 2 hours or more. Enjoy as is or pour the ganache over the chilled brownies and refrigerate to set and serve. Just before serving, garnish with pomegranate arils.

Chocolate Ganache

Makes enough for an 8-inch square pan

1 cup (8 ounces) 72% or higher dark chocolate squares

2 tablespoons coconut oil

2 tablespoons almond or coconut milk

In a double boiler, place all of the ingredients and heat over low heat until fully melted. Stir until the mixture is smooth and thickens slightly. Great for topping Raw Brownies (page 110) and other desserts.

Cinnamon-Rooibos Cake

Makes one 9-inch two-layer cake

Oprah Winfrey said, "The more you praise and celebrate your life, the more there is in life to celebrate." For those special moments that make life amazing, I have a cake recipe that will delight and excite all your senses and that's good for you, too. Yes, all this is possible!

Cinnamon and rooibos are rich in antioxidants and polyphenols and flavonoids. I know you don't care about all that when you bite into a slice of cake, but just knowing that it's good for you is reason enough to celebrate. This cake is also gluten-free, dairy-free, egg-free, and nut-free. Because food intolerances and allergies are on the rise, it's nice not to leave anyone behind. But beyond all this goodness, this cake is stunning from the first bite to the last crumb. Make it as a simple sheet cake for a weekend treat or double the recipe for an impressive four-layer special-occasion cake. There are always good reasons to enjoy some cake!

1¾ cups all-purpose gluten-free flour or light spelt flour

2 teaspoons ground cinnamon

1 tablespoon raw cacao powder

1 tablespoon baking powder

¾ cup coconut palm sugar

¼ teaspoon fine sea salt

¾ cup unsweetened applesauce

½ cup brewed rooibos tea

½ cup grapeseed oil

Real Strawberry Frosting (page 118) made without the strawberries

Fresh blueberries, for topping (optional)

Fresh mint sprigs, for topping (optional)

Sift the flour, cinnamon, and cacao and baking powders into a bowl. Add the sugar and salt and mix to combine.

In another bowl, combine the applesauce, tea, and oil and pour into the dry ingredients, mix well. Let stand for 10 to 15 minutes.

Meanwhile, preheat the oven to 375°F and line two cake pans with parchment paper.

Distribute the batter evenly in the two pans and bake on the middle rack for 15 to 18 minutes, until a toothpick comes out dry. Let rest for 2 to 3 minutes, then remove the cakes from the pans, remove the parchment paper while hot, and set aside to cool.

Continued

To assemble, work with room-temperature cake and cold frosting. First, spread some frosting on your platter to hold the cake in place. Level the cake layers with a serrated knife (except the top layer). Frost the top of the bottom layer. Stack the second layer onto the frosting and repeat. Finally, frost the sides, if desired. Top with blueberries and mint leaves.

NOTE If making a 4-layer cake (as shown in the photo), double the recipe for the cake and frosting and distribute the batter evenly over 4 pans. You can also bake one layer at a time with a fresh sheet of parchment paper each time; just be sure to divide the batter accordingly.

Vanilla Cupcakes
with Real Strawberry Frosting

Makes 12 cupcakes

They say cupcakes are happiness, and sometimes it's true! I love to celebrate special occasions in style. Birthday parties are my favorite—they're all about the pretty details and delicious food. I enjoy making birthday cakes and other desserts from scratch because it's important to me to know what my kids and their friends eat is of the best quality. Just the thought of store-bought treats makes me cringe. I can't believe all the sugar and artificial and unhealthy ingredients. Food coloring and sprinkles (which are made almost entirely of food coloring and sugar) are my biggest pet peeves! That's why these vanilla cupcakes are so wonderful. They are delicious and festive, all without any gluten or artificial ingredients.

1¾ cups all-purpose gluten-free flour or light spelt flour

1 tablespoon baking powder

½ cup powdered stevia

¼ cup raw cane sugar

¼ teaspoon sea salt

¾ cup unsweetened applesauce

½ cup hot water

½ cup coconut oil, melted, or grapeseed oil

1 tablespoon vanilla extract

Real Strawberry Frosting (recipe follows) or Sweet Potato and Date Chocolate Frosting (recipe follows)

Sift the flour and baking powder into a large bowl. Add the stevia, sugar, and salt and whisk to combine well. In a separate bowl, combine the applesauce, water, oil, and vanilla.

Pour the liquid mixture into the dry ingredients and mix with a wooden spoon to combine well until a smooth batter forms. Let the batter rest for about 20 minutes.

Preheat the oven to 375°F and line a 12-cup muffin pan with paper liners.

Scoop or pour the batter into the paper liners to fill three-quarters full. Bake for 25 to 30 minutes, until golden on top and a toothpick inserted into the center comes out clean.

Leave the cupcakes to cool for about 10 minutes in the pan, then transfer to a cooling rack and allow to cool completely, for a total of 1 hour. Frost as desired.

If baking gluten-free, this recipe is best enjoyed the same day.

Real Strawberry Frosting

Makes enough for 12 cupcakes

This frosting recipe is especially fun. Puréed fresh strawberries are the secret to a burst of flavor and color, no food coloring or sprinkles required.

½ cup almond milk, cold

1 tablespoon potato starch

2 tablespoons raw cane sugar

¾ cup organic vegan buttery spread

¼ cup vegan shortening

15 to 20 drops liquid stevia

1½ cups fresh strawberries, puréed smooth and chilled

In a small saucepan, mix the almond milk with the potato starch until completely dissolved. Add the sugar and continuously stir over low-medium heat until completely dissolved. Do not bring to a boil. Continue stirring for about 1 minute more, or until the mixture thickens to a pudding texture. Remove from the heat and allow to cool. Store in the refrigerator until ready to make the frosting. (The mixture can be kept refrigerated for up to 3 days.)

In a stand mixer, whip the vegan butter and shortening on high speed until light and fluffy, about 5 minutes. Slowly add the milk mixture, one spoonful at a time, while continually mixing. Add the stevia and continue mixing for a few more minutes, turning the mixer off a few times to scrape the sides of the bowl. Check for sweetness and add more sweetener if desired. (I personally like the frosting only a little sweet, as the cake is also sweetened.) If the frosting has warmed up and gone soft, chill in the refrigerator until it becomes cold again, about 30 minutes or more. (You can make the frosting up to 3 days ahead.)

Just before frosting, whip in the strawberry purée and incorporate well, about 5 minutes. Spread or pipe on top of the cupcakes or other desserts.

NOTE I keep my vegan shortening and vegan butter in the freezer so they stay fresher longer, and take out enough for a recipe at a time.

Sweet Potato and Date Chocolate Frosting

Makes enough for 12 cupcakes

This chocolate frosting is so smooth and delicious. Best of all, it's made from surprisingly simple and wholesome ingredients. For a big time-saver, use leftover sweet potatoes or cook more and keep for dinner. This chocolate frosting is also great to eat on its own, like a pudding.

1 cup peeled and cooked sweet potato

8 Medjool dates, pitted

2 tablespoons raw cacao powder

Process the sweet potato and dates in a food processor on high speed to a smooth paste. Add the cacao powder and continue processing until well incorporated. Spread or pipe onto the cupcakes or other desserts. Store in a sealed container in the refrigerator. Use within 3 days.

Simply Divine Raw Chocolate Truffles

Makes 12 truffles

Truffles have always been my guilty pleasure. I had a thing for a box of dark chocolate truffles with ice wine on special occasions. But nights like that can only last for so long. Now I prefer healthier options like this one. Thanks to the great ingredients, I can enjoy myself even more because I know I won't suffer a headache or tummy ache, or look pregnant the next day!

½ cup raw walnuts

½ cup raw pecans

½ cup raw cashews

1 cup packed Medjool dates, pitted

1 teaspoon vanilla extract

3 tablespoons raw cacao powder

Pinch of sea or Himalayan pink salt

½ cup (4 ounces) unsweetened dark chocolate

10 to 20 drops liquid stevia

Place all of the nuts in a food processor and grind until crumbs form. Add the dates, vanilla, cacao powder, and salt and continue mixing until smooth.

Scoop about a teaspoon of the mixture onto the palm of your hands and roll into walnut-size balls. Continue with all the dough.

Melt the chocolate in a double boiler over low heat and sweeten with liquid stevia to your liking. Roll the balls to coat all over. Place on a parchment-lined flat surface and place in the freezer for about 10 minutes to set.

Store in an airtight container in the refrigerator for up to 1 week or freeze to have a healthy dessert on hand.

Chocolate-Cherry-Chia Pudding

Serves 2

Cherries and chocolate! This has been my most divine dessert combination for years, and it's delightful to embrace these decadent flavors guilt-free. You will not believe the incredible taste of this pudding. I don't even know how to fit the words *rich*, *decadent*, and *healthy* into the same sentence—just take my word that this dessert is completely good for you in every way. Yes, you could have it for breakfast. And yes, you can go back for seconds!

1½ cups nondairy milk (almond, coconut, and hemp are my favorites)

¼ cup chia seeds (look for ground chia seeds if you prefer a smooth texture)

3 tablespoons raw cacao powder

5 drops liquid stevia or 2 to 3 tablespoons date or rice malt syrup

½ cup cherries, pitted and sliced, plus whole cherries for serving

Cacao nibs, for topping

Dark chocolate shavings, for topping (use 70% or higher dark chocolate) (optional)

In a bowl or Mason jar, stir together the milk, chia seeds, and cacao powder and refrigerate for at least 4 hours or overnight. Mix again and sweeten with stevia as desired.

Just before serving, divide the mixture among serving dishes and top with the sliced cherries, cacao nibs, whole cherries, and chocolate shavings for that extra indulgence.

NOTE Cherries are naturally very sweet, which is why I prefer to sweeten this pudding with stevia to cut the sugar calories but not the sweetness.

PROTEIN CHOCOLATE CHIP COOKIES

Makes 12 cookies

Who doesn't love chocolate chip cookies? I remember a time when I could go through a bag of them. I didn't even want to eat them all, but they had their way with me and I felt so darn helpless. But now I'm stronger and wiser. The secret is in these ingredients. It's easy to overeat empty carbs because you don't feel satiated, so you keep going. But when you add protein, you feel full after one or two cookies and you naturally don't crave as many. No one will guess the secret ingredient here—they're that delicious!

1½ cups cooked chickpeas (1 19-ounce can), rinsed and drained

½ cup almond butter or sunflower butter

2 tablespoons rolled oats

½ teaspoon baking powder

¼ teaspoon fine sea salt

¼ cup coconut nectar or maple syrup

1½ teaspoons vanilla extract

2 to 4 drops liquid stevia (optional)

½ cup mini dark chocolate chips

Preheat oven to 350°F and line a baking sheet with parchment paper.

Combine the chickpeas, almond butter, oats, baking powder, salt, coconut nectar, and vanilla in a food processor and mix until all the ingredients are incorporated. Scrape the sides of the bowl, add the stevia, if using, and process again until a smooth batter forms. Fold in the chocolate chips by hand.

Scoop about 1 tablespoon of the batter per cookie onto the baking sheet (you can place these quite close together, as they do not spread) and bake for 12 minutes, or until they look dry and lightly browned on top.

Allow to cool for about 8 minutes on the baking sheet. Enjoy while still warm. Store in an airtight container at room temperature for up to 3 days or in the refrigerator for up to 1 week.

Raw Amaretto-Clementine Cheesecake

Serves 4

Cheesecake used to be my guilty pleasure . . . and still is. But now I enjoy indulging in these cashew-based "cheesecakes" that are so much healthier and more delicious. You can't go wrong with pure, amazing ingredients. These have a date-sweetened almond base with a rich, creamy cashew cheese center and are topped with delicious amaretto-stewed clementines. When made in mini Mason jars, these make great portable picnic desserts!

Crust

¾ cup raw almonds

½ cup raw pecans

½ cup Medjool dates, pitted

½ teaspoon vanilla extract

Pinch of Himalayan pink salt

1 teaspoon water

Filling

2½ cups raw cashews, soaked in water for at least 2 hours

¼ cup maple syrup or coconut nectar

2 tablespoons freshly squeezed lemon juice

Juice of 2 clementines, or 4 drops natural orange essential oil in ¼ cup water

6 drops liquid stevia

½ cup coconut oil, melted

Amaretto Clementines (recipe follows)

Fresh mint leaves, for garnish

For the crust: Place the almonds and pecans in a food processor and mix on high speed until they turn into flour. Add the dates, vanilla, and salt and continue mixing until well combined. If mixture is too crumbly and does not stick between your fingers, add a teaspoon of water and mix again.

Press into the bottom of 4 short jars—mini Mason jars work great. (Or press into an 8-inch parchment-lined springform pan to make a single large cake.)

For the filling: Rinse and drain the cashews, put them in the food processor, and process on high for a few minutes to make fine crumbs. Add the maple syrup, lemon juice, clementine juice, stevia, and coconut oil. Continue processing on high until very smooth. Scoop or pour over the crust.

If making the cheesecakes in jars, cover with parchment paper or plastic wrap (not the Mason jar lids) and place in the freezer to set for 4 hours, then move to the refrigerator 1 hour before serving.

When ready to serve, top with the amaretto clementines and fresh mint.

Amaretto Clementines

Makes 1/2 cup

6 clementines, peeled and segmented

1 teaspoon vanilla extract

1 teaspoon amaretto extract or amaretto liqueur

1 tablespoon coconut oil

Heat a medium skillet over medium heat and add the clementine segments, vanilla, amaretto extract, and coconut oil. Stir often so they don't burn and cook for about 5 minutes, or until juices seep out and the clementines are soft. Turn off the heat and let cool. Serve warm or chilled over the cheesecakes, or over ice cream, waffles, or pancakes.

CHOCOLATE-DIPPED ALMOND & CACAO NIB BISCOTTI

Makes 24 biscotti

Once upon a time I liked to play housewife. I cleaned the house while I danced and sang, I bought fresh flowers along with the groceries, and I baked every Sunday. My husband and I lived in a small apartment by the lake, just the two of us. Homemade biscotti were his favorite, and I mastered a traditional recipe we both enjoyed very much. That was before the whirlwind of events that shook up my health and our marriage.

More recently, when I set out ingredients for this flourless and eggless version, those honeymoon days came to mind. This recipe reminds me that you can always live the sweet life—daydream, have fresh flowers, dance in the kitchen, and enjoy good coffee and biscotti with your best friend. Nowadays we share these with the little ones and drop-in guests, and it's even better.

4 cups almond flour

2 tablespoons arrowroot or tapioca starch

1 teaspoon baking soda

½ teaspoon sea salt

½ cup coconut nectar or maple syrup

2 teaspoons almond extract

½ cup raw almonds, chopped

½ cup raw cacao nibs

½ cup unsweetened dark chocolate, for dipping (optional)

5 to 10 drops liquid stevia

Preheat the oven to 350°F and line a baking sheet with parchment paper.

Whisk the flour, starch, baking soda, and salt in a bowl. Mix in the coconut nectar and almond extract. Fold in the almonds and cacao nibs. Halve the dough and roll into logs about 3 inches wide, 12 to 14 inches long, and 2 inches high.

Bake the logs for 14 to 20 minutes. Remove from the oven and let cool for 10 minutes. In the meantime, lower the oven temperature to 250°F.

Slice the logs on the diagonal ¾-inch thick. Place the biscotti flat on the baking sheet. Bake for 10 minutes on each side.

Melt the chocolate in a double boiler, add the stevia, to taste, stir to combine, and dip the bottom of each biscotti. Place in the fridge to set, about 10 minutes. Store in an airtight container at room temperature for up to 1 week (if they last this long).

Peanut Butter Cookies, Two Ways

Makes 15 to 20 cookies

Peanut butter cookies are such perfection. It was my mission to reinvent them from healthier ingredients so my daughter could have a great nutritious snack after school.

These are so delicious as raw cookies, but you can also bake them. Both are tested and both are awesome—I guess it all depends on your patience level. The raw version makes soft, chewy cookies; the baked version makes for firmer, crunchier cookies.

1 cup almond flour

4 Medjool dates, pitted

⅓ cup peanut butter

¼ teaspoon baking soda

¼ teaspoon fine sea salt

2 tablespoons grapeseed or coconut oil

1 teaspoon vanilla extract

If baking the cookies, preheat the oven to 350°F and line a baking sheet with parchment paper.

Mix all of the ingredients in a food processor until a smooth dough forms. Roll into golf ball–size balls in the palms of your hand and place on a parchment-lined baking sheet about 2 inches apart. Press down gently to flatten, then indent the top with a fork. Serve raw just like that.

For a baked version, place on the baking sheet and bake for 12 minutes, until slightly golden. Remove from the oven and allow to cool on the baking sheet. (This is very important, as they will crumble when they are still hot.) Enjoy once fully cooled. Store in an airtight container in the refrigerator for up to 7 days. These freeze well, too.

Raw Chocolate-Dipped Maca-roons

Makes 15 to 20 macaroons

These maca-roons are such delights! The name is a bit of a play on words, since these raw, egg-free macaroons are taken to the next level with the addition of the amazing superfood maca! Best of all, they're quick, easy to make, and have a whole lot of good stuff in them.

2 cups unsweetened coconut flakes

½ cup almond flour

2 to 3 teaspoons maca powder

5 tablespoons coconut oil

¼ cup raw honey or coconut syrup

1 teaspoon vanilla extract

Pinch of sea salt

½ to 1 teaspoon water

¼ cup 72% or higher dark chocolate

Mix the coconut flakes, almond flour, maca powder, honey, vanilla, and salt in a food processor until a smooth dough forms. The dough should stick together when pressed. If it's too crumbly, add the water and mix more.

Roll into golf ball–size balls in the palms of your hand and flatten just the bottoms onto a parchment-lined tray or baking sheet that fits in your refrigerator or freezer.

Melt the chocolate in a double boiler and dip the bottom of each macaroon into the chocolate. Set on the prepared tray and place in the refrigerator for 30 minutes or the freezer for 5 minutes to set. Store in an airtight container in the refrigerator or at room temperature for up to 7 days.

 NOTE Maca is not recommended for children, so this is an adults-only treat.

Vanilla Bean–Coconut Ice Cream

Serves 4 to 6

Coconut ice cream is a godsend. I used to marvel over the intricate art of ice cream making—it can be such a complicated task when you make it the traditional way (with eggs and heavy cream), but hello! This vegan version keeps things simple with only one main ingredient. It's clean ice cream, without any bad stuff and only the good stuff. Because sometimes you have to uncomplicate things in life.

2 cans full-fat coconut milk, at room temperature

2 tablespoons tapioca starch or arrowroot

2 tablespoons maple syrup or coconut nectar

2 tablespoons coconut oil

2 teaspoons vanilla bean paste or vanilla extract

10 to 20 drops liquid stevia

Combine the coconut milk with the starch in a small saucepan and whisk until fully combined. Place over medium heat and add the maple syrup and coconut oil while stirring continuously until it starts to thicken, about 5 minutes. Remove from the heat and whisk in the vanilla and stevia to taste. Allow to cool completely and then refrigerate until the mixture is fully cold, at least 2 hours.

Transfer the cold coconut mixture to an ice cream maker and proceed according to the manufacturer's instructions. Enjoy immediately, or freeze in an airtight container for up to 1 month. If freezing, allow to rest at room temperature for 10 to 15 minutes to thaw slightly before serving.

NOTE To prevent freezer burn, cut a piece of parchment paper the size of the container and stick it onto the top of the ice cream, pressing down to get as much air out as possible.

Raw Berry Swirl Cheesecake

Makes one 10-inch cake

When you celebrate life and special occasions, make those moments meaningful and delicious. But more than that, make them with no boundaries, no restrictions, or guilt.

Allergies, intolerances, and tummy aches are no fun and shouldn't have to cross anyone's mind during a celebration. A cake that omits all the bad stuff and radiates pure beauty with healthy, delicious, beautiful ingredients keeps everyone happy. That's the real celebration—feeling carefree because you know you're enjoying the best of the best!

Crust

2 cups raw almonds

1 cup raisins

Pinch of Himalayan pink or fine sea salt

Filling

3 cups raw cashews, soaked in water for 2 to 4 hours

¾ cup honey or coconut nectar

¾ cup coconut oil, melted

Juice and zest of 1 lemon

2 cups fresh strawberries or other red berries, like raspberries, plus more for garnish

2 cups fresh blueberries or other dark berries, like blackberries, plus more for garnish

For the crust: Line a 10-inch springform pan with parchment paper cut to size.

In a food processor, grind the almonds into flour. Add the raisins and salt and continue blending until well combined. Add a little water, blending until the mixture sticks together when pressed. Press evenly into the bottom of the pan and set aside.

For the filling: Rinse and drain the cashews and grind in the food processor until fine crumbs form. Add the honey, coconut oil, and lemon zest and juice and continue blending until smooth. Be sure to stop occasionally to scrape down the sides of the bowl.

Transfer about two-thirds of the cashew mixture to a bowl. Add the strawberries to the remaining one-third of the cashew mixture and blend until smooth. Transfer this strawberry mixture to a bowl. Scoop half of the plain cashew mixture back to the food processor, add the blueberries, and blend until smooth. Now you have three colors of cheesecake.

To make the swirls, alternate spreading a few tablespoons of each color cheesecake mixture onto the crust at a time until all the mixture is used. Place in the freezer for 4 to 6 hours or overnight. Transfer to the refrigerator at least 6 hours before serving. Serve cold, topped with extra berries.

Raw Raspberry-Lemon Mini Cheesecakes

Serves 12

Raspberries and lemon just go together! This raw cheesecake is scrumptious, and it's made with the best good-for-you ingredients. It's also quick to make and just needs a couple of hours to set, so if you have guests coming soon, there's still time to make them!

Crust

¾ cup raw almonds

½ cup Medjool dates, pitted

¼ cup naturally sweetened dried cranberries

Pinch of sea salt

Filling

2 cups raw cashews, soaked in hot water for 1 to 2 hours (or refrigerate overnight in cold water)

½ cup coconut oil, melted but not hot

½ cup coconut nectar or light maple syrup

¼ cup water

Zest and juice of 1 lemon, plus more zest for garnish

Fresh raspberries, for serving

Fresh mint leaves, for garnish

NOTE If you're using zest in any recipe, be sure to buy organic lemons. If you can't get organic lemons, pour boiling water over the lemon to melt the waxy coating (which is often petroleum-based). Do this two more times and wipe well when the lemon is still hot. This will remove a lot of the coating.

For the crust: In a food processor, pulse the almonds until finely ground. Add the dates, cranberries, and salt. Continue mixing until the mixture sticks together in your fingers. (Be sure to turn off the processor each time you check, and always scoop with a spoon!) If it's too dry, add water 1 tablespoon at a time (up to 2 tablespoons). Once it sticks together and still falls off your fingers, it's perfect. Wipe the food processor with a paper towel and return to its stand.

Press the mixture evenly into the bottoms of a 12-cup silicone muffin pan and set aside.

For the filling: Rinse and drain the cashews. Add the cashews, coconut oil, coconut nectar, water, and lemon zest and juice to the food processor again and mix on high for about 5 minutes, or until very smooth.

Pour the filling evenly over the crusts. Tap the pan gently to settle. Place in the freezer for 1 to 2 hours. Thaw slightly (5 to 10 minutes) in the refrigerator before serving. Top with fresh raspberries, lemon zest, and mint leaves. Enjoy! The cheesecakes will keep, tightly wrapped with plastic wrap, in the freezer for up to 1 month.

SUPERFOOD CHOCOLATE THINS

Makes 30 to 40 pieces

I am a chocoholic. It's true. I've always been and probably always will be. But I've learned what sets good chocolate apart from the rest. It's all about the quality. And I have learned to have treats in moderation. When you work with pure, high-quality ingredients, you create a treat that's full of antioxidants, superfood power, and other delicious, natural, amazing things. These are so quick and fun to make (and eat!). But be careful, they can be addictive. Consider yourself warned.

¾ to 1 cup (7 to 8 ounces) 72% or higher dark chocolate squares

¼ cup coconut oil

2 tablespoons raw cacao powder

Topping Combinations

Pumpkin seeds and shelled hemp seeds

Chia seeds and puffed millet

Sunflower seeds and dried goji berries

Unsweetened coconut flakes and raw cacao nibs

All kinds of chopped raw nuts, such as almonds, hazelnuts, and Brazil nuts

Line a flat tray or baking sheet (that fits into your freezer) with parchment paper.

Using a double boiler, melt the chocolate over low heat. Add the coconut oil and cacao powder and mix until smooth.

Scoop or pour onto the parchment-lined tray and sprinkle with your favorite toppings. To make several flavors in one go, I scooped the chocolate into separate "puddles" and sprinkled on my favorite toppings. Place in the freezer for at least 30 minutes, or until set. Break into pieces and enjoy. Store in the freezer in an airtight container with parchment paper between the layers. Keeps well for up to 1 month.

Stewed Strawberries

Makes 1 cup

There's nothing more delicious than warm, aromatic strawberries to top your waffles, pancakes, pie, or ice cream. So good and naturally sweet.

1 pint fresh strawberries, hulled and sliced

Cook the strawberries in a medium skillet over medium heat for about 10 minutes, or until the strawberries soften and the juices are oozing out. If the strawberries stick or start to burn, add a few tablespoons of water and mix. Add more water (up to ¼ cup) if it cooks off quickly. Purée if a sauce is desired.

Serve on desserts, oatmeal, ice cream, yogurt, or whatever you like. Store in an airtight container in the refrigerator for up to 1 week.

 NOTE This is a great recipe for any berries or fruit that are not at peak freshness and to save very ripe fresh fruit before it goes bad.

No Bake Chocolate Mocha Cake

Serves 6

This tiramisu-inspired cake is absolute perfection! It goes great with a good cup of coffee or chai tea.

Mocha Layer

2½ cups raw walnuts (or a mix of walnuts and pecans)

5 Medjool dates, pitted

¼ cup coconut nectar or maple syrup

4 drops liquid stevia

¼ cup raw cacao powder

Cashew Layer

2 cups raw cashews, soaked in water at least 2 hours or overnight

¼ cup coconut oil, melted

¼ cup coconut nectar or maple syrup

¼ cup coffee, brewed and cold (optional)

1 teaspoon vanilla extract or vanilla bean paste

Pinch of Himalayan pink salt

Chocolate Ganache (page 112), for topping

Whipped Coconut Milk (page 10), for serving

Raw cacao nibs, for serving

Line a 4 by 9-inch loaf pan with parchment paper, making sure the paper extends above the sides so it's easy to pull out the cake.

To make the mocha layer: Grind the walnuts in a food processor to a fine texture. Add the dates, coconut nectar, stevia, and cacao powder and mix on high until the dates are broken down completely. The texture should remain crumbly; do not overmix. Press half of this mixture evenly and firmly into the bottom of the pan. Transfer the remaining mixture to a bowl and set aside.

To make the cashew layer: Wipe the food processor clean with a paper towel. Rinse and drain the cashews well, and grind to a fine texture in the food processor. Add the coconut oil, coconut nectar, coffee, vanilla, and salt and process on high until smooth. Spread half of this mixture on the mocha layer in the pan. Place the pan in the freezer to set, about 2 hours. Keep the remaining mixture in the refrigerator.

Remove the pan from the freezer and top with the remaining mocha mixture, pressing evenly and firmly. Smooth the remaining cashew mixture on top. Pour the ganache over the top, spreading with a spatula. Return to the freezer to set another 2 hours or overnight. To serve, soften in the refrigerator for 2 hours or at room temperature for 30 minutes.

Serve with Whipped Coconut Milk and cacao nibs.

Two-Ingredient Peanut Butter Cups

Makes 10 to 12 cups

Move over, Reese's—these homemade peanut butter cups are way better! They contain only two clean ingredients (plus one optional one), and they're really quick and easy to make.

7 ounces 72% dark chocolate squares, or 1 cup vegan chocolate chips

¼ cup coconut oil, optional

About ¾ cup all-natural peanut butter or sunflower butter

Melt the chocolate in a double boiler. Turn off the heat and leave on the burner to keep warm. (For added healthy fat benefits and a delicious hint of coconut, melt coconut oil into the chocolate. You can do the same with the peanut butter if you like.)

Line a flat dish with 10 to 12 cupcake liners. Scoop a tablespoon of melted chocolate into each. Place in the freezer for about 2 minutes to set. Remove from the freezer and add a teaspoon of peanut butter in the center and gently flatten with the back of a spoon. Spoon more melted chocolate to cover the peanut butter (1 to 2 tablespoons). Return to the freezer for about 15 minutes to set. They are best when the peanut butter filling is soft, not frozen, and the chocolate outside is crispy.

Chocolate Mousse Tart with Chocolate Chip Cookie Crust

Serves 6 to 8

I love homemade desserts that are quick, delicious, and impressive. This tart takes my cookie recipe and turns it into a stunning chocolate tart with little effort. Top with seasonal fruit for that extra sweetness and natural beauty. It's chocolate decadence to live for!

Protein Chocolate Chip Cookie dough (page 125)

¾ cup (6 ounces) dark 80% chocolate squares or chocolate chips

½ cup coconut oil

1 cup raw cashews, soaked in water for at least 2 hours

¼ cup water, warmed

Fresh berries, for serving (optional)

Fresh mint sprigs, for serving (optional)

Preheat the oven to 350°F. Line the bottom of a 10-inch tart pan with parchment paper and grease the sides.

Press the cookie dough evenly in the baking dish, pushing the dough up the sides. Bake for 12 to 15 minutes, until golden on top. Remove from the oven and allow to fully cool.

In the meantime, melt the chocolate in a double boiler over low heat, stirring occasionally. In another small pot, heat the coconut oil until it's fully melted but not boiling. Turn off the heat once it's melted.

Rinse and drain the cashews and process on high speed in a food processor. Add the melted chocolate, coconut oil, and warm water. Process until the ingredients are fully mixed, turning off the processor and scraping down the sides of the bowl to get all the ingredients.

Pour the mousse over the chocolate chip cookie base and place in the refrigerator to set for about 2 hours. To serve almost immediately, place in the freezer for about 5 minutes, or until fully set. Top with fresh berries and mint.

COCONUT-VANILLA DOUGHNUTS

Makes 6 to 8 doughnuts

It's true doughnuts have a bad reputation, but what's not to love? It's a round, fluffy cake with a hole in the center! Adorable, is it not? Doughnuts are especially tasty when you create them with great ingredients such as gluten-free flour, applesauce, coconut oil, and coconut milk.

1½ cups all-purpose gluten-free flour

½ cup raw cane sugar

½ cup powdered stevia

1½ teaspoons baking powder

¼ teaspoon baking soda

¼ teaspoon sea salt

½ cup coconut milk

⅓ cup coconut oil

½ cup unsweetened applesauce

1 teaspoon vanilla extract

1¼ cups unsweetened coconut flakes, divided

½ cup rice malt syrup

2 tablespoons coconut oil, melted

Preheat the oven to 350°F. Grease and flour a 6-well doughnut pan.

In a large bowl, sift together the flour, sugar, stevia, baking powder, baking soda, and salt.

In a medium saucepan, warm the coconut milk and oil over low heat until the oil melts (do not allow to boil), mixing gently with a wooden spoon. Remove from the heat and stir in the applesauce and vanilla.

Pour the liquid mixture into the dry ingredients and mix gently. If clumps develop, use an immersion blender or mixer and mix until very smooth. Stir in ½ cup of the coconut flakes. Pour the batter into the doughnut pan, filling about halfway to allow for rising.

Bake for 15 minutes. Remove from the oven and allow to cool for 15 to 30 minutes. Gently scrape the sides of each well and flip the pan to turn the doughnuts out. Use a toothpick to help them lift out if needed.

Spread ¼ cup coconut flakes on a plate. In a small bowl mix the rice malt syrup and coconut oil together until well combined. Coat the doughnuts thinly with the icing and press onto the remaining ½ cup coconut flakes to coat all over.

MINT CHOCOLATE PUDDING

Serves 1

With just a few ingredients, you can make a great little treat. I happen to have these ingredients at home all the time. (I recommend that, too!)

Purchasing pudding is just forbidden in our house. Both my daughter and I just love fresh homemade pudding—it really is easy, quick, and delicious.

2 cups almond milk or other nondairy milk

2 tablespoons coconut sugar, date sugar, or raw cane sugar

2 tablespoons coconut oil

3 tablespoons raw cacao powder

1 tablespoon potato starch

1 tablespoon arrowroot

½ teaspoon mint extract

4 to 6 drops liquid stevia

Dark Chocolate Cups (optional; recipe follows)

NOTE Serve the pudding in small bowls or chill in the refrigerator for about 30 minutes to serve in the dark chocolate cups for double chocolatiness!

In a small saucepan over medium-low heat, heat 1½ cups of the almond milk with the sugar and coconut oil, stirring occasionally. Do not bring to a boil.

While the milk is warming, fill a cup with the remaining ½ cup almond milk. Add the cacao powder, potato starch, and arrowroot and stir well to break up clumps. (It helps to use the back of a spoon and press any clumps against the sides of the cup. If necessary, you can use an immersion blender for a few seconds.)

Slowly pour the cacao-milk mixture into the saucepan on the stove, mixing rapidly to combine. Once incorporated, keep mixing slowly for 2 to 3 minutes while the pot is still over the heat. Stir in the coconut oil mixture. The mixture will begin to thicken and will resemble a pudding. Remove from the heat and stir in the mint extract and stevia. Allow to stand for a few minutes to cool slightly. You may serve this pudding still hot or cold—it all depends on how you personally like it.

Serve the pudding in small bowls or chill in the refrigerator for about 30 minutes to serve in the dark chocolate cups for double chocolatiness!

Dark Chocolate Cups

Makes 12 to 15 cups

I love that I can whip up a quick and easy dessert for those days when we want a little something sweet. You can take my Mint Chocolate Pudding (page 153) to the next level and serve it in these chocolate cups.

1 cup (7 ounces) 72% or higher chocolate squares

NOTE Great for filling with fresh fruit, too! Use unsweetened chocolate and add stevia to taste to lower the sugar calories even further.

Melt the chocolate in the top of a double boiler. Pour into a silicone muffin pan and swirl to coat the wells up the sides and as evenly as possible. Place in the freezer for 5 minutes to set. If little holes appear, pour more melted chocolate to create a double coat where needed and place back in the freezer. Remove from the freezer when set (about 30 minutes) and pop the cups out by pushing the bottoms of the silicone wells.

Raw Chocolate Sauce

Makes 1/2 cup

Drizzle this sauce over fruit or parfaits, stir it into chia pudding, dip fruit into it and then place in the freezer to harden—the possibilities for this sauce are endless. Enjoy with caution!

6 tablespoons coconut oil

¼ cup raw cacao powder

2 tablespoons almond or coconut milk

3 to 4 tablespoons coconut nectar or liquid stevia

Melt the coconut oil in a small saucepan over low heat and stir in the cacao powder and milk, stirring until the mixture thickens slightly. Remove from the heat and pour into a serving dish. Stir in coconut nectar to taste.

Snacks

TURNIP THE BEET CHIPS

Serves 1 to 4 (depending on self-control, appetite, and selfishness)

Turn up the beat with these delicious and colorful vegetable chips. These are way healthier than potato chips, and making them at home is easy and fun. Best of all, you get to eat chips! Yay!

4 turnips, peeled

4 beets, peeled

¼ cup grapeseed oil or neutral oil of your choice

1 teaspoon sea salt

Preheat the oven to 325°F and line a baking sheet with parchment paper.

Slice the turnips and beets using a mandoline and place in a large bowl. Drizzle the oil over the vegetables, sprinkle with the salt, and toss to coat all over.

Bake for 15 minutes, turning over halfway through the baking time. Then lower the temperature to 200°F and bake for another 5 to 10 minutes, until nice and golden.

Raw Cheesy Kale Chips

Serves 2

Sometimes snacking on chips isn't about the actual chips—it's about that snacking experience of reaching for a salty, crunchy bite! Change your habit to kale chips and you can keep snacking, but on better food. Makes sense, right?

Bunch of kale, stemmed

1 cup raw cashews, soaked in water for at least 2 hours

½ red or orange bell pepper

2 cloves garlic, peeled

¾ cup water

Juice of ½ lemon

2 tablespoons nutritional yeast flakes

½ teaspoon sea salt

Preheat the oven to 300°F and line a baking sheet with parchment paper.

Make sure the kale leaves are thoroughly dry. Tear the leaves into large pieces and place in a large bowl. Rinse and drain the cashews.

In a food processor, process the cashews, bell pepper, garlic, water, lemon juice, yeast flakes, and salt until a smooth paste forms.

Toss the kale leaves in the paste to coat all over. Place on the baking sheet in a single layer, being sure to not overlap.

Bake for 15 minutes, then flip the leaves and bake for another 10 minutes. Remove from the oven and allow to cool for 5 minutes before devouring!

NOTE Alternatively, you can dehydrate the kale leaves in a food dehydrator for 8 hours on a high setting (no need to turn them over).

Raw Cranberry-Chocolate Protein Balls

Makes 20 balls

I don't like to skip meals, and I take my between-meals snacks very seriously. These protein balls are a healthy snack disguised as a dessert. These are my go-to snacks post-workout, on busy days, or just when I'm out and about. I love this combination of nuts, cacao, and cranberries. The additional protein in them is what will make you feel full and help you avoid a sugar crash. So important!

1½ cups raw walnuts

1 cup raw pecans

½ cup naturally sweetened dried cranberries

5 Medjool dates, pitted

¼ cup raw cacao powder

1 to 2 tablespoons chocolate or vanilla protein powder

1 to 2 teaspoons water

1 teaspoon vanilla extract

4 drops liquid stevia

Process all of the ingredients in a food processor until a dough forms.

Turn off the food processor, remove the blade, and roll a teaspoon of the dough in the palms of your hands into a ball. Repeat with all the dough. That's it! Enjoy between meals or after a workout. Store in an airtight container in the refrigerator for up to 1 week or in the freezer for up to 3 months.

Two-Ingredient Cookies

Makes 15 to 20 cookies

Sometimes all you really want is a cookie—am I right? These cookies keep it healthy, delicious, easy, and very simple. After all, you can't get any simpler than two ingredients. You can also really customize these to your liking by adding in chocolate chips, nuts, seeds, and spices. Have fun!

2 very ripe bananas

1 cup rolled oats

Add-ins

¼ cup dark chocolate chips or dried fruit, nuts, hemp, or sunflower seeds

1 teaspoon ground cinnamon

Preheat the oven to 350°F and line a baking sheet with parchment paper.

In a bowl, squish the bananas with a fork. Add the oats and mix until fully incorporated.

Scoop about 1 tablespoon of batter per cookie onto the baking sheet. Bake for 13 to 15 minutes, until golden.

Allow to fully cool before serving.

SUPERHERO BARS

Makes 9 squares

For years, I was addicted to store-bought granola, energy, and protein bars—they satisfied my sweet tooth, and I thought they were healthy. But it turns out that even some "quality" granola and energy bars have over 20 grams of sugar apiece. And even though they may seem like healthier sugars, now I know better. I like my bars to have lots of vitamins, minerals, protein, and be completely organic, tasty, and low in sugar!

This is a recipe I make when we are packing for a road trip or about to hop on an airplane or just simply run short of healthy fuel on busy days. They keep well for up to three weeks, and you can freeze them to have a stash always on hand. (They travel well.) Yes, they are real superheroes!

2 tablespoons ground flax seeds or chia seeds

6 tablespoons water

⅓ cup Medjool dates, pitted, soaked in warm water if they need softening

2 cups gluten-free rolled oats

½ cup hemp hearts (shelled hemp seeds)

2 tablespoons whole hemp seeds (optional)

2 tablespoons sunflower flour or sunflower seeds

3 tablespoons raw cacao powder

1 to 2 teaspoons ground cinnamon

½ teaspoon Himalayan pink or fine sea salt

¾ cup unsweetened applesauce

⅓ cup maple syrup or rice malt syrup

¼ cup coconut oil, melted

2 teaspoons vanilla extract

Preheat the oven to 350°F. Line a 9-inch baking pan with enough parchment paper to extend above the sides.

In a small bowl, mix the flax seeds with the water and set aside for 5 minutes.

In a food processor, process the dates into a paste, then add the oats and mix again. Add all of the remaining ingredients and process just to combine.

Press the mixture evenly into the pan, pressing down firmly with your hands or the back of a wooden spoon. Smooth the top. If the mixture sticks, wet the spoon with a little water.

Bake for 15 minutes, until top darkens slightly. Let cool about 10 minutes. Remove from the pan and slice. Serve while still warm (if you can't wait) or store in an airtight container in the refrigerator for up to 3 weeks. These also freeze well in a freezer bag with parchment paper between the bars for up to 3 months.

PURE STRAWBERRY POPS

Makes 4 to 6 pops

The perfect way to cool off! Of course, we all love the fresh abundance of fresh local fruits and veggies in summer, especially yummy berries. These are so easy to make, and it's pure joy to see your own wholesome ingredients go into them.

1 pint fresh strawberries, hulled

1 cup coconut water

2 tablespoons honey or stevia (optional)

Purée the strawberries and coconut water in a blender. Turn off the blender and taste the mixture. It may be sweet enough for you. If not, add the sweetener a little bit at a time.

Pour the purée into ice pop molds and freeze for at least 4 to 6 hours, or preferably overnight.

Citrus & Pomegranate Salad

Serves 2

The citrusy, minty freshness of this salad is just incredible and really wakes you up! Not to mention that it's so healthy—full of vitamin C, beta-carotene, fiber, antioxidants, and lots more good stuff.

1 pink grapefruit, peeled

2 or 3 clementines, peeled

Arils from ½ pomegranate

Fresh mint leaves, for serving

Cut the grapefruit into chunks and slice the clementines into round slices so they look pretty in a wide serving bowl. Sprinkle the pomegranate arils on the grapefruit and clementine slices, top with fresh mint leaves, and serve.

 NOTE My favorite way to remove the arils from a pomegranate is to submerge it in a bowl of cool water and cut and pull apart the pieces under water. I have tried many methods, and this is the only way I have found to keep the juices away from clothes and the surrounding area. Then drain the arils and enjoy, mess-free!!

Apple-Cinnamon Fruit Leather

Makes 12 strips

Homemade fruit leather is the best candy ever. You can make so many variations with different fruit for all kinds of different flavors. It's so easy to make and such a great treat for kids and adults alike!

2 cups applesauce (homemade, or unsweetened if purchased)

½ teaspoon ground cinnamon

1 tablespoon ground flax seeds (optional)

Mix the applesauce and cinnamon in a bowl. If adding flax seeds, set aside for 15 minutes.

To make using a dehydrator: Spread an even layer of the apple-cinnamon mixture about ⅛ inch deep onto drying sheets. Turn the dehydrator on to the lowest setting and heat for 8 to 10 hours, until it's no longer sticky and peels off easily.

To make using an oven: Spread an even layer about ⅛ inch deep onto a baking sheet lined with a silicone baking mat sheet. Bake at 150°F (or your lowest setting) for 6 to 8 hours, until the top is no longer sticky and is dry to the touch. Remove and let cool completely.

For easier handling and storage, cut a sheet of parchment paper the same size and transfer the fruit leather onto it. Cut the fruit leather (and paper) into strips 1 to 2 inches wide with a sharp knife, kitchen scissors, or pizza cutter. Store in an airtight container for up to 3 weeks.

NOTE You can use any soft-flesh fresh fruit, such as strawberries or other berries, bananas, peaches, or mango (peeled and pitted).

HOMEMADE FRUIT ROLL-UPS

makes 12 strips

The flavors really intensify when you dry fruit, so you don't need additional sugar. I also find that organic fruit is so much sweeter—it's like biting into nature's candy! Use a single fruit, or experiment with different combinations.

2 cups soft-flesh fresh fruit, such as strawberries and other berries, bananas, peaches, or mango, peeled and pitted

1 tablespoon ground flax seeds (optional)

In a food processor, purée the fruit with the flax seeds until smooth.

To make using a dehydrator: Spread an even layer of the fruit mixture about ⅛ inch deep onto drying sheets. Turn the dehydrator on the lowest setting and heat for 8 to 10 hours, until it's no longer sticky and peels off easily.

To make using an oven: Spread an even layer about ⅛ inch deep onto a baking sheet lined with a silicone baking mat sheet. Bake at 150°F (or your lowest setting) for 6 to 8 hours or overnight, until the top is no longer sticky and is dry to the touch. Remove and let cool completely.

For easier handling and storage, cut a sheet of parchment paper the same size and transfer the fruit leather onto it. Cut the fruit leather (and paper) into strips 1 to 2 inches wide with a sharp knife, kitchen scissors, or pizza cutter. Store in an airtight container for up to 3 weeks.

 NOTE You don't need the flax seeds in this recipe, but I like the extra nutritional boost they provide. You can't even taste them!

HOMEMADE KETCHUP

Makes 1 cup

Making your own ketchup is easier than you think, especially if you cut corners and use tomato paste. This way you can avoid the GMO high-fructose corn syrup added to most commercial ketchup.

2 (6-ounce) cans tomato paste

2 tablespoons raw apple cider vinegar

1 tablespoon blackstrap molasses

1 tablespoon maple syrup

½ teaspoon garlic powder

½ teaspoon onion powder

½ teaspoon sea salt

Mix all of the ingredients in a bowl until well combined. Store in an airtight container in the refrigerator for up to 1 week. If it thickens too much for your taste, mix in a little water just before serving.

Healthy Three-Ingredient Chocolate Pudding

Serves 1

What do you do when those chocolate cravings take over and you feel like you're about to lose it? Make this instead. I promise it's just like chocolate but even better (and better for you)!

1 ripe banana

1 teaspoon raw cacao powder

½ teaspoon ground cinnamon

Slice the banana into a serving bowl, add the cacao powder and cinnamon, and mash with a fork or blend with an immersion blender. Serve immediately.

CHIA PUDDING

Serves 1 or 2

Chia pudding is such a great way to maximize nutrition in a very simple way. Once you get into the habit of devoting all of 2 minutes in the evening to make it up, you will be able to enjoy it for a healthy breakfast or snack the next day. Chia pudding also makes a great post-workout snack, as it's naturally rich in protein and has lots of superfood nutrition. Because this version is naturally sugar-free, it also makes a great evening snack. Basically, you'll soon discover it's the best thing ever with just three ingredients!

¼ cup chia seeds

1 cup almond milk or other nondairy milk

2 to 3 drops liquid stevia

Fresh fruit of your choice, for topping (optional)

In a small bowl or Mason jar, whisk the chia seeds with the almond milk and place in the refrigerator for about 4 hours, or up to overnight. Stir it occasionally, as the chia seeds will settle at the bottom.

Sweeten with stevia to taste and serve with fruit, if using.

CASHEW CHEESE BALL

Serves 4 to 8

Making your own cheese ball from cashew nuts is incredibly easy and so delicious—and so healthy. This is a great addition to a party buffet table. You and your guests will love it. It goes well with Superseed Flax Crackers (page 169).

2 cups raw cashews, soaked in water for at least 2 hours or overnight

2 tablespoons nutritional yeast flakes

1 teaspoon miso paste

1 clove garlic, peeled

2 tablespoons freshly squeezed lemon juice

1 tablespoon dried basil or dill

1 teaspoon onion powder

1 teaspoon sea salt

½ teaspoon freshly ground black pepper

¼ teaspoon cayenne pepper (optional)

Handful of finely chopped raw almonds or pine nuts or handful of chopped fresh herbs, such as chives, for topping

Rinse and drain the cashews. Place in a food processor and process on high speed until crumbs form. Add the yeast, miso paste, garlic, lemon juice, basil, and onion powder, and mix on high speed to make a smooth paste. Season with the salt, black pepper, and cayenne.

Transfer the mixture to a cheesecloth. Wrap the cheesecloth around the mixture, forming it into a ball, and twist the top, squeezing out as much moisture as possible. Tuck the ends of the cheesecloth underneath the ball and place it in a colander. Suspend the colander in a larger bowl and transfer the bowl to the refrigerator for 2 hours, until the liquid no longer drips and the ball holds its shape.

Sprinkle the nuts on a plate. Unwrap the cheese ball and roll in the chopped nuts until fully encrusted. Serve with Superseed Flax Crackers (page 169).

Drinks

The Green Super Smoothie

Serves 2

This super smoothie is my go-to for proper nourishment on those days when I'm busy or just feel like I could use a nutritional boost. It's filled with vitamins, minerals, protein, and even probiotics.

2 cups almond milk or hemp milk

1 large ripe banana

1 cup loosely packed spinach

1 tablespoon hemp hearts (shelled hemp seeds)

1 tablespoon chia seeds

1 capsule probiotic (acidophilus-bifidus mix)

In a blender, mix all of the ingredients. Serve immediately.

BLACKBERRY-SPIRULINA SMOOTHIE

Serves 2

A delicious smoothie filled with antioxidants, calcium, potassium, vitamin C, fiber, omega-3 fatty acids, vitamin K, and iron. Okay, so what's the lowdown of that list? It's excellent for mood boosting!

2 ripe bananas

1½ to 2 cups flax milk or other nondairy milk

Handful of fresh blackberries

2 teaspoons ground chia seeds

1 teaspoon spirulina powder

1 teaspoon rice protein powder (optional)

In a blender, mix all of the ingredients. Serve immediately.

STRAWBERRY-SPINACH ENERGY SMOOTHIE

Serves 2

On those days when you need a boost of energy, here's the smoothie you want.

2 cups coconut water

1 cup fresh strawberries, hulled

Handful of baby spinach

1 to 2 teaspoons maca powder

2 drops liquid stevia (optional)

In a blender, mix the coconut water, strawberries, spinach, and maca powder. Check for sweetness and add stevia a drop at a time, to your liking. Serve immediately.

 NOTE Use frozen fruit for a more refreshing icy beverage. Maca is not recommended for children.

Pineapple-Coconut Smoothie

Serves 2

Pineapple and coconut make me think of the beach and sunshine every time (even in the winter). This smoothie is a delicious escape that bursts with sweetness and is so refreshing—and healthy, too!

1½ cups coconut water

½ cup almond or coconut milk

1 cup fresh pineapple chunks

1 to 2 teaspoons chopped fresh ginger

In a blender, mix all of the ingredients. Serve immediately.

NOTE Fresh pineapple becomes sweeter as it ripens. For best results store the pineapple in a paper bag on the kitchen counter to ripen evenly. I like to cut into mine when the flesh becomes a bit soft to the touch.

Fruit-Infused Water

Serves 1

Infuse your water with a few pieces of fruit (fresh or frozen) and voilà: delicious water with vitamins and natural sugars. It's a fun variation if you get tired of plain old H$_2$O. The possibilities are endless here, so use your imagination!

1 cup filtered water

Handful of fresh or frozen berries or chopped fruit and/or fresh herbs, such as mint or basil

Pour the water into a bowl and add the fruit and herbs. Let stand for 2 hours at room temperature or overnight in the refrigerator.

Fruit Ice Cubes

Fruit-infused ice cubes are a great idea for summertime barbecues and parties. You get super-cute, fun, healthy add-ins to your drinks! Simply pour the water into an ice cube tray and drop in various berries—raspberries, blueberries, blackberries, or cranberries—as well as herb leaves such as mint or rosemary. Serve the ice cubes in still or sparkling water.

ACKNOWLEDGMENTS

Sometimes the stars align, and all your wishes come true. I keep pinching myself that this book is real, and this is not just a dream. When you believe in yourself, work hard, and create with passion, amazing things happen! This book is beyond my dreams, and I am so thankful to some amazing people for making *Cut the Sugar* possible.

To Coleen O'Shea, my wish-upon-a-star agent, thank you so much from the bottom of my heart for first, finding me and believing in me from the start, and for your patience and guidance in this whole process. Without you this book would not be possible.

To Grace Suh, senior editor at Andrews McMeel, for being so wonderful and patient and understanding of a new writer with a baby at her side. Your guidance, support, and expertise have been exceptional.

To everyone else at Andrews McMeel: Holly Ogden, art director; Maureen Sullivan, copy chief; Carol Coe, production manager; Andrea Shores, cookbook publicist; and Kate Morin, social media and online marketing coordinator, for offering so much insight and support and who worked so hard to get this book out to the world, my deepest gratitude for the whole team.

To my blog readers, for your continued support and cheerleading along my healing and blogging journey. I am so happy to share recipes that you find delicious and healthy. Thank you for sharing your joy with *Pure Ella* recipes through comments, e-mails, and photos. This book would not be possible without you. To the amazing blogging community for inspiring me on this amazing journey. I am learning so much every day from such great and talented people. I am grateful to call some of you my friends (too many to list), but you know who you are. Thank you for your support over the years and helping *Pure Ella* grow.

To my sweet friend and recipe tester, Kristine Warman, for enjoying *Cut the Sugar* recipes so much, giving me a boost of confidence, and making me smile by sharing how happy your family is while enjoying so many recipes from the book. I am so thankful for your tips and suggestions.

To Blynda DaCosta, for her beautiful photography (pages 66–67).

To my mom, who always puts others' needs in front of hers and is always patient and kind. Without your help and support this book would not have been possible. Love you, Mamusia!

To my husband—my manager, my rock, and my confidence booster: Thank you for your patience and support. Nineteen years strong; 10 years in marriage, in sickness and in health, in good times and in bad, we have lived through so much of a whirlwind, but you are my wind beneath my jumpsuit. Thanks for being a great daddy to our children and for putting up with me all these years.

To my kids: Gabriella, you are the coolest kid and a very creative future writer—Grace will know what to do with your talents! You're so big now but Mommy can hold you in her arms anytime you want!

Thanks, honey, for understanding why Mommy's been so busy and for being an amazing big sister. Amelia, sweetie, thank you for all the baby smiles and giggles Mommy's needed these last few months. You made this process so much fun!

To my sisters, Kasia and Barbara, for helping me SO much to make this book possible. Your support, assistance, and love is so appreciated. I am so grateful for you ladies and for my whole family for helping me these last few months.

I have learned so much in these last few years: to never give up on yourself and to keep doing what you love. To not be afraid of trying new things and to live and create with passion. I wish this for all my readers.

To the stars: for shining bright for me. To the universe: for catching me each time I fall.

METRIC CONVERSIONS & EQUIVALENTS

METRIC CONVERSION FORMULAS

TO CONVERT	MULTIPLY
Ounces to grams	Ounces by 28.35
Pounds to kilograms	Pounds by .454
Teaspoons to milliliters	Teaspoons by 4.93
Tablespoons to milliliters	Tablespoons by 14.79
Fluid ounces to milliliters	Fluid ounces by 29.57
Cups to milliliters	Cups by 236.59
Cups to liters	Cups by .236
Pints to liters	Pints by .473
Quarts to liters	Quarts by .946
Gallons to liters	Gallons by 3.785
Inches to centimeters	Inches by 2.54

APPROXIMATE METRIC EQUIVALENTS

VOLUME

¼ teaspoon	1 milliliter
½ teaspoon	2.5 milliliters
¾ teaspoon	4 milliliters
1 teaspoon	5 milliliters
1¼ teaspoons	6 milliliters
1½ teaspoons	7.5 milliliters
1¾ teaspoons	8.5 milliliters
2 teaspoons	10 milliliters
1 tablespoon (½ fluid ounce)	15 milliliters
2 tablespoons (1 fluid ounce)	30 milliliters
¼ cup	60 milliliters
⅓ cup	80 milliliters
½ cup (4 fluid ounces)	120 milliliters
⅔ cup	160 milliliters
¾ cup	180 milliliters
1 cup (8 fluid ounces)	240 milliliters
1¼ cups	300 milliliters
1½ cups (12 fluid ounces)	360 milliliters
1⅔ cups	400 milliliters
2 cups (1 pint)	460 milliliters
3 cups	700 milliliters
4 cups (1 quart)	0.95 liter
1 quart plus ¼ cup	1 liter
4 quarts (1 gallon)	3.8 liters

LENGTH

⅛ inch	3 millimeters
¼ inch	6 millimeters
½ inch	1¼ centimeters
1 inch	2½ centimeters
2 inches	5 centimeters
2½ inches	6 centimeters
4 inches	10 centimeters
5 inches	13 centimeters
6 inches	15¼ centimeters
12 inches (1 foot)	30 centimeters

WEIGHT

¼ ounce	7 grams
½ ounce	14 grams
¾ ounce	21 grams
1 ounce	28 grams
1¼ ounces	35 grams
1½ ounces	42.5 grams
1⅔ ounces	45 grams
2 ounces	57 grams
3 ounces	85 grams
4 ounces (¼ pound)	113 grams
5 ounces	142 grams
6 ounces	170 grams
7 ounces	198 grams
8 ounces (½ pound)	227 grams
16 ounces (1 pound)	454 grams
35.25 ounces (2.2 pounds)	1 kilogram

OVEN TEMPERATURES

To convert Fahrenheit to Celsius, subtract 32 from Fahrenheit, multiply the result by 5, then divide by 9.

DESCRIPTION	FAHRENHEIT	CELSIUS	BRITISH GAS MARK
Very cool	200°	95°	0
Very cool	225°	110°	¼
Very cool	250°	120°	½
Cool	275°	135°	1
Cool	300°	150°	2
Warm	325°	165°	3
Moderate	350°	175°	4
Moderately hot	375°	190°	5
Fairly hot	400°	200°	6
Hot	425°	220°	7
Very hot	450°	230°	8
Very hot	475°	245°	9

Information compiled from a variety of sources, including *Recipes into Type* by Joan Whitman and Dolores Simon (Newton, MA: Biscuit Books, 1993); *The New Food Lover's Companion* by Sharon Tyler Herbst (Hauppauge, NY: Barron's, 2013); and *Rosemary Brown's Big Kitchen Instruction Book* (Kansas City, MO: Andrews McMeel, 1998).

INDEX

Andrews McMeel Publishing, LLC
an Andrews McMeel Universal company
1130 Walnut Street, Kansas City, Missouri 64106

www.andrewsmcmeel.com

16 17 18 19 20 SHO 10 9 8 7 6 5 4 3 2 1

ISBN: 978-1-4494-7071-5

Library of Congress Control Number: 2015945001

Editor: Grace Suh
Art director: Holly Ogden
Copy chief: Maureen Sullivan
Production manager: Carol Coe
Demand planner: Sue Eikos

Photography on pages 66–67
by Blynda DaCosta.

ATTENTION: SCHOOLS AND BUSINESSES
Andrews McMeel books are available at quantity discounts with bulk purchase for educational, business, or sales promotional use. For information, please e-mail the Andrews McMeel Publishing Special Sales Department: specialsales@amuniversal.com